RE-IM

Mothering
& Career

INSIGHTS FROM A
TIME OF CRISIS

**JENNA A. LOGIUDICE, EVELYN BILIAS LOLIS,
AND KATHRYN E. PHILLIPS**

DEMETER

Re-imagining Mothering & Career
Insights from a Time of Crisis

Jenna A. LoGiudice, Evelyn Bilias Lolis, Kathryn E. Phillips

Copyright © 2023 Demeter Press

Demeter Press
PO Box 197
Coe Hill, Ontario
Canada
K0L 1P0
Tel: 289-383-0134
Email: info@demeterpress.org
Website: www.demeterpress.org

Demeter Press logo based on the sculpture "Demeter" by Maria-Luise Bodirsky www.keramik-atelier.bodirsky.de

Printed and Bound in Canada

Cover design: Evelyn Bilias Lolis
Typesetting: Michelle Pirovich
Proof reading: Jena Woodhouse

Library and Archives Canada Cataloguing in Publication
Title: Re-imagining mothering and career: insights from a time of crisis / edited by Jenna A. LoGiudice, Evelyn Bilias Lolis, and Kathryn E. Phillips.
Names: LoGiudice, Jenna A., editor. | Bilias Lolis, Evelyn, editor. | Phillips, Kathryn E., editor.
Description: Includes bibliographical references.
Identifiers: Canadiana 20230486223 | ISBN 9781772584639 (softcover)
Subjects: LCSH: Working mothers—United States. | LCSH: Working mothers—United States—Anecdotes.
Classification: LCC HQ759.48 .R45 2023 | DDC 306.874/30973—dc23

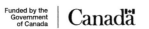 The publisher gratefully acknowledges the support of the Government of Canada

Acknowledgements

We wish to acknowledge and provide our sincere appreciation to the Fund for Women and Girls of Fairfield County's Community Foundation (FCCF) for their support and unwavering trust in the meaningfulness of this project and what it will bring to both local groups, and to broader communities of mothers; and to the Fairfield University Mu Chi Chapter of Sigma Theta Tau for their recognition of the importance of this book to add to the literature on mothers with careers and re-imagining a path forward.

About the Authors

Jenna A. LoGiudice, PhD, CNM, RN, FACNM is an Associate Professor and the Midwifery Program Director at Fairfield University's Egan School of Nursing and Health Studies. She has been providing midwifery care since 2008. She worked as a full scope certified nurse midwife in Waterbury, CT, providing holistic care to families. She now continues to attend births through her per diem midwifery position on labor and birth at Yale New Haven Hospital. In her professional roles, Dr. Jenna LoGiudice values shared decision making with her patients and students. Her research centers the importance of trauma-informed care. She is the mother of four incredible kids and to keep up with them is an avid exerciser. In her free time, she enjoys being at the beach and outdoors in nature with her family. Of all her titles, mother is unrivaled.

Evelyn Bilias Lolis, PhD, is the Interim Dean and Associate Professor of School Psychology and Special Education for Fairfield University. She has worked in child mental health for twenty years designing various therapeutic programs and offering ongoing consultations for positive psychological interventions in the schools. Dr. Evelyn is an educational psychologist, interventionist, wellness advisor, and blogger. Her scholarship is in the area of connectedness, resiliency, wellbeing, and inclusion. As a board director for Hellenic Professional Women, Dr. Evelyn spearheads their women's wellness series. She has been interviewed extensively on parenting during the pandemic and has hosted numerous professional seminars on resiliency, wellbeing, and self-compassion for parents, schools, corporate professionals, and executive women. She is mother to two beautiful twin girls.

Kathryn E. Phillips, PhD, RN, APRN, and CHSE, is an Associate Professor in the Egan School of Nursing and Health Studies at Fairfield University. As a nurse, she has worked in a variety of settings including long-term care, acute care, and home care. In her academic role, Dr. Phillips enjoys teaching and mentoring students, especially guiding them through the research process. She strives to support each individual on their path of flourishing through a focus on holistic wellness, along with being a present and connected mother to four energetic kids.

Contents

The world woke me one morning
With a reality surreal
And expected me to mother,
And work,
And stay real

The world woke me one morning
With the tug of a child
And pulled me to the window
As if snow
Had laced the ground

The world woke me one morning
With the kiss of change
Uninvited and undeniable
The world I once knew
Would fade

The world woke me one morning
With an opportunity askew
To look at myself closely
The old,
And the new.

Preface

As three women who mothered and maintained careers during the pandemic, we often found ourselves within our social circles recounting the trials, tribulations, and lessons from this time. It is no secret that mothering involves perpetual self-reflection and re-counting. The insights afforded on these pages did not come without a cost: sleepless nights, worry about our own and our family's health, and relentless recounting—recounting of decisions, recounting of options, recounting of possibilities, and the brutal recounting of self as we toggled between work and mothering, often feeling no separation between the two.

The SARS-CoV-2, COVID-19 pandemic fundamentally shook us to the core. It also forced us to explore what adaptations and transformations emerged as a result of this period. In this way, this book weds the historical account of the period with that of a trajectory toward healing and restoration. Our conversations focussed on what we as working mothers chose to hold on to and retain from our former way of life and what we elected to let go of or shed as a result of the experience of living, working, and mothering during a global health crisis.

We invite you to read this book, which is a window into the hearts of diverse mothers working and mothering during a time of crisis. It is a kaleidoscope of learnings, vulnerabilities, and hopes. These narratives are real, raw, and emotional. Individually, they represent the tenacity of the human spirit. Collectively, they offer a lens toward restoring a more integrated, holistic self—a way to re-imagine mothering and career.

We, the authors, have witnessed that letting go of what no longer serves us, our families, and careers is just as much a part of the healing process as deciding what parts of ourselves to faithfully preserve. Our insights gleaned shine through with new meaning and perspective. Fundamentally, our own paths to restoring how we live as working mothers exposed us to the humble realization that we need not go back to life as it was in all ways. We hope the same will hold true for you as well.

In rebuilding, we found ourselves asking the vital question: "How exactly can we heal after a time of chronic stress and adversity?" The process of restoration is an ever delicate one. Think of a vintage piece of furniture, an old photo, or a piece of artwork. Restoration involves salvaging what is notable, usable, and appreciated about an item and then fusing it with the visionary—how it can be enhanced, what it can become. Much like the image on the cover of this book representing the Japanese art form *Kintsugi* (Richman-Abdou), we are not disguising the cracks brought on by this pandemic. Rather, we are mindfully welding the old with the new—a mosaic reimagination of the mothers we are and the mothers we aspire to be.

The aim of this book is to bring to light the shared consciousness of motherhood, a common veil that transcends time, space, region, and boundary. We hope you find these lessons to be timeless, validating, and additive to your role as a mother who maintains a career while raising a family. We encourage you to read each essay with an openness of heart, finding perhaps a small piece of yourself in each narrative. We are optimistic that you will embrace what speaks to your soul and, moreover, feel validated and deeply empowered as you read. For this purpose, you will find a series of reflective prompts at the end of each chapter for your review. We welcome you to reflect on these questions and apply the related exercises in ways that relate to your circumstance and life. We hope the insights extracted from the narrative accounts as well as these self-reflective prompts help to promote meaning as well as personal and professional growth. This book invites you on a journey to explore the ways in which we as women have found our way through a time of crisis amid all our roles.

Works Cited

Richman-Abdou, Kelly. "Kintsugi: The Centuries-Old Art of Repairing Broken Pottery with Gold." *My Modern Met*, 5 Mar. 2022, https://mymodernmet.com/kintsugi-kintsukuroi/. Accessed 23 May 2023.

Introduction

L ife is about constant change; at times, this change accelerates at a rapid pace. In 2020, when the world came to a grinding halt, life was forever altered. Daily existence changed in a moment, creating a collision of our expectations and reality. The rhythm of our routines ended, as we adapted to the current state of affairs and the ever-looming unknown. Expectations could not be clearly defined as the world shutdown. External forces were making decisions that abruptly altered our daily plans, causing our minds to spiral with many uncertainties. When will my kids return to school? Do I need to wear a mask? Are my family members safe? What if I get sick? What if I need to choose between home and work? These questions occupied our minds in addition to the day-to-day concerns that had to be dealt with, such as safely feeding our families and providing stability for our children at a time when they were suffering from a disruption in their normal routine without answers about what the future would hold.

Among the most affected by the dramatic shift in life events were mothers (Croda and Grossbard 7). As the heart of the family system, mothers provide support, protection, and love. They supply the emotional glue that binds each member of the family together, regulates children's mood states, and supports their loved ones through thick and thin. Although a mother's work can be overlooked by society, it is found in the very fabric of her family's daily life. Mothers care deeply, and this emotional work increased dramatically when the pandemic hit. Devoting more time to the emotional lives of their children and ensuring their wellbeing, mothers were called to provide more for their families.

Additionally, another alteration in mothers' work was the increase in the physical care they had to provide for their children during their working hours. Mothers were now responsible for overseeing their children's education and daily care, as schools and daycares shut down. For mothers who had careers, this meant they had to maintain their jobs and regular household duties while adding on childcare and educational responsibilities. Mothering now required exponentially more energy, physical effort, and emotional reserves than before the pandemic.

As if this intense level of mothering was not enough, there was also the increased mental load of constant decision making in the context of changing health regulations. Each decision required mothers to evaluate the available choices through the lens of a potential health threat. Every professional event, playground trip, and family gathering was filtered through one fundamental question: "Is this a safe choice for my family in light of the pandemic?" Humans are social creatures, surviving through interdependence on one another. The drive for social connection is wired into our bodies, providing emotional and physical health benefits (Martino, Pegg, and Pegg Frates 466). COVID-19 had attacked our human nature, causing us to weigh the risks and benefits of physical illness with the need for human connection. This new mental layer viciously seeped into everyday matters and directly placed two human drives in competition with each other.

The days turned into weeks, weeks into months, and months into years. Motherhood and careering were suspended in a state of perpetual flux as schools and daycares opened and closed. All the while there was the sobering reality that the boundaries between home, work, and self were elusively dissipating. The added stress, without easy ways to get support, was stretching women thin and causing burnout (Aldossari and Chaudhry 831; Lakshmin). With more to do, wage-earning mothers had less time than usual to ensure their personal needs were met. Without time to address their own wellness, something had to give: We cannot provide from an empty tank.

The precautionary message to always remember to put your own oxygen mask on first before helping to stabilize others—a travel metaphor that had been utilized pre-pandemic as an analogy for self-care—did not translate to the pandemic. It appeared as if everyone's masks —those for mothers themselves, their partners, their children, and their work colleagues—were all left dangling just out of reach. How does one recalibrate in this case? As you will witness in the upcoming chapters, mothers did anything and everything they could to preserve themselves, their families, and their career responsibilities. Each one did so in her own unique way, yet they were collectively a part of a larger mothering narrative.

A crisis is the standstill at which the schism of the old is forced to stare squarely at the prospect of the new. The shattering of the old is the apex of any crisis. A breaking point provides an opportune moment for growth while also requiring a shedding of the familiar and status quo —the old. In this way, a crisis forces the core elements of an individual's identity to be re-evaluated. We have to fall into uncertainty, be vulnerable, and be uncomfortable because the outcome is unclear. Just as a caterpillar enters a chrysalis, completely dissolves into a biological mush of potential, and re-emerges as a beautiful butterfly, the pandemic created an opportunity for career mothers. Mothers with careers were offered the chance to take the dark days of the pandemic and assemble a life filled with choices that aligned with their core values.

Enter not only the "great resignation"—a pandemic period coined by the career industry with inordinately high turnover and early retirement of women especially (Fuller and Kerr)—but also the "great renegotiation," a time of calling for improved working conditions and lifestyles (Women in Revenue). Who led the great resignation? Women. Some did so by choice, others because there was no other option but to resign because of responsibilities at home. Mothers, once again, were left to absorb the brunt of the traumatic shock of a crisis period. Who started and continues to lead the great renegotiation? Women again. They stood up to collectively demand increased pay, more fulfillment, and better environments for the workplace.

Although breaking points are uncomfortable, they provide an opening in more ways than one. They are personal and individual, yet there are similarities across what all wage-earning mothers were facing at these breaking points during the pandemic. This breaking allowed each individual to reassess why they were doing things a certain way, if what they were doing held meaning, and if what they were doing was worth the time and energy they put into it. The cross section of priorities and personal/familial values was laid on the table in pieces of brokenness begging for revival.

Hence, the disruption of the COVID-19 pandemic resulted in many women who were mothering and careering to reflect on what was most important to them and how they wanted their life to look going forward. This journey, albeit unique to every woman, was commonly fraught with sobering moments of brokenness, despondency, fragility, and, ultimately, the resilience to carry on, to share, and to grow. Providing a distinctive chance to examine their goals and design a path to get there, mothers courageously seized the opportunity to re-imagine their lives. Brokenness became the catalyst and the driver.

The re-envisioned and redesigned ideas about mothering and career presented in this book are born out of the rapid change brought on by a global pandemic. Once something is broken apart, it can be reassembled in a new way. The pieces, born out of the shattering, are available for building in any number of ways; they present an opportunity to create without limitations, as all possibilities are presented. This re-imagining of new possibilities brings us back to the Kintsugi art (Richman-Abdou) —pieces that are not only re-imagined and brought together but infused with gold to expose the process, the nonlinear pathway to a re-imagined state. As mothers, we too can create a more perfect future by assembling the pieces of our life into a beautiful work of art that reflects where we have been and where we want to go.

As the COVID-19 pandemic has impacted every facet of a mother's work, life, and career, it has further pronounced the flaw in our system: an expectation and bias from society that mothers should carry it all and wear it well. The pandemic brought forth a new challenge of both mothering and holding onto a career. When the world was turned upside down by a global pandemic, mothers were asked to steadfastly be there for their families and to maintain a career. Change is difficult, yet often when challenged the most, one emerges with the deepest of insights. This book will explore the narratives and self-realizations of women across a wide range of ages, backgrounds, disciplines, and circumstances. Thoughtful. Insightful. Honest. Painstakingly real. Documenting this experience as it was lived by career mothers—women who were working and mothering during this time—empowers the voices of all women whose stories live in the common humanity detailed in this contemporary anthology.

We hope that you can join us in celebrating the great rebirth of the female spirit and find value and meaning in hearing the stories of others who navigated their way through this challenging time. The reflective prompts provided at the end of each chapter are there to help you consider how you can apply the wisdom of these mothers to your own circumstance. As Cleary Vaughan-Lee reminds us, "When we remember a story that touches our hearts, we reflect on what it means to be human. We can then decide how we want to live and be in the world."

Works Cited

Aldossari, Maryam, and Sara Chaudhry. "Women and Burnout in the Context of a Pandemic." *Gender Work, & Organization,* vol. 28, no. 2, 2020, pp. 826-34.

Croda, Enrica, and Shoshana Grossbard. "Women Pay the Price of COVID-19 More Than Men." *Review of Economics in the Household,* vol. 19, 2021, pp. 1-9.

Fuller, Joseph, and William Kerr. " The Great Resignation Did not Begin with the Pandemic." *Harvard Business Review,* 23 Mar. 2022, https://hbr.org/2022/03/the-great-resignation-didnt-start-with-the-pandemic. Accessed 25 May 2023.

Lakshmin, Pooja. "The Primal Scream. How Society Has Turned Its Back on Mothers. This Isn't Just about Burnout, It's about Betrayal." *New York Times,* 4 Feb. 2021, https://www.nytimes.com/2021/02/04/parenting/working-mom-burnout-coronavirus.html. Accessed 25 May 2023.

Martino, Jessica, Jennifer Pegg, and Elizabeth Pegg Frates. "The Connection Prescription: Using the Power of Social Interactions and the Deep Desire for Connectedness to Empower Health and Wellness." *American Journal of Lifestyle Medicine,* vol. 11, no. 6, 2017, pp. 466-75.

Richman-Abdou, Kelly. "Kintsugi: The Centuries-Old Art of Repairing Broken Pottery with Gold." *My Modern Met.,* 5 Mar. 2022, https://mymodernmet.com/kintsugi-kintsukuroi/. Accessed 25 May 2023.

Vaughan-Lee, Cleary. "Grateful Changemakers: Global Oneness Project." *Grateful,* https://grateful.org/grateful-changemakers/grateful-changemakers-global-oneness-project/ Accessed 8 June 2023.

Women in Revenue. "The Great Renegotiation: The Definitive 2022 State of Women in Revenue Report." March 2022, https://staticl.

squarespace.com/static/5d1536430653fc00012a48f7/t/6245f
85654aefd2c8b035a98/1648752727570/WIR_eBook_Defini-
tive_2022_Report_Final-3-29.pdf?utm_campaign=WIR+eBook.
Accessed 25 May 2023.

Chapter 2

Tapestry

It is imperative to provide a window into the thirty-three female contributors who have been gracious with their time and energy to share their pandemic experiences, insights, and awakenings throughout this book. We were intentional to invite and to include women in a wide array of careers, who have children of all ages, and represent varied ethnicities and family structures. Twenty-seven percent of the women who shared their stories are from diverse ethnicities, representing Black, Latina, Asian, and Middle-Eastern cultures; and 30 percent are part of varied family compositions, including single mothers, same-sex mothers, stepmothers, divorced mothers, and a widowed mother. Their children range in age from newborns through teenagers, with some contributors having given birth during the pandemic. These mothers range in age from their early thirties through their fifties and represent a multitude of careers: educators, small business owners, healthcare providers, probation and police officers, hairstylists, personal trainers, a lawyer, an animator, and a doula. This is in no way an exhaustive list yet provides a starting point for further reflection, discussion, and sharing.

We asked these women in the winter of 2021-2022 to contribute an essay focused on what their life was like at the start of the pandemic in 2020 and what insights from this time have emerged for them personally. What we could not have known when we invited them to write was that in January of 2022, as many were still writing, that another wave of the pandemic would brutally affect day-to-day life in the United States (US). So, while these women were writing about their experience at the start of the pandemic, it is important to contextualize the world around them when they contributed. Additionally, because these women reside in various regions of the US (from Connecticut, to the Midwest, to California), we also must contextualize the responses to the pandemic —such as the exact times of lockdowns, mask mandates, and school closures—which differed from state to state.

These women were asked to contribute because they were employed in wage-earning jobs at the onset and throughout the pandemic. In this way, these mothers experienced the pandemic in a manner that demanded they both meet the unpaid work needs of their homes and the responsibilities of their wage-earning jobs.

We have purposely included a varied sample of contributors and voices to help you, the reader, have the opportunity to both relate and grow from these shared experiences. We, the authors, certainly and humbly have grown through their stories and wisdom. As you read and reflect, we gently remind you that each individual has contributed a narrative that depicts their own lived experience of mothering and working through the pandemic. We invite you to read with respect for what each voice brings to the table of motherhood. It is our sincere hope that through diversity of industry, family composition, ethnicity, and race you will find inspiration, a voice that resonates, and most importantly, personal empowerment and validation.

Chapter 3

Compassion for Self

Being human is not about being any one particular way;
it is about being as life creates you.

—Kristen Neff

In the psychological literature, self-compassion is the ability to treat oneself with the same kindness, compassion, and mercy you would show a good friend experiencing a similar hardship, stressor, or struggle (Neff and Germer). It is the ability to evaluate stress, struggle, or disappointment with nonjudgment and approach personal shortcomings with tenderness. The awakenings of the following essays provide a glimpse of the ways these six mothers discovered how to walk in discomfort and brave imperfection with openness and grit. Their professions were three first responder advanced practice nurses; two university professors, one educator for students with special needs and one senior scientist researcher; and an appellate court attorney. Two of these women were mothers to four young children aged seven and under; one became pregnant and endured pregnancy during the pandemic; one was a single mother educator who was responsible for her child's education; and one had two elementary-school-aged children, who also became responsible for their education.

The following accounts, though varied in experience and circumstance, speak to the realization that mothers cannot and should not be held to unrealistic and inequitable standards for meeting the demands of motherhood and professional work.

The Sand in Your Hand

Life is a balance of holding on and letting go.

—Rumi

I've found that life is about striving for balance, often among things that may appear disparate. For example, wanting to be close to my children while also needing time for myself. An analogy for this equilibrium is sand in your hand. It is a balance of active acceptance —holding your fingers together while not gripping tightly—that allows the sand to remain steadily placed. If you loosen your fingers or squeeze too hard, the sand will slip away.

As a goal-driven person, I've often found it hard to let it go. I also constantly strive for balance in all areas of my life. When the pandemic began, my children were little (six months, four and five years). My husband and I were fortunate to have jobs that allowed us to continue working through the pandemic. This was burned in my mind as I watched friends and neighbors who were laid off or furloughed during the pandemic shutdown. Gratitude was my guide as we struggled through the enormous workload of balancing two careers and childcare without help or daycare. There was little time for reflection or self-care. Things were completely out of balance. I was struggling to create stability for myself and the children. As the pandemic wore on, it became clear this would be a long duration event. We had to find a way to live with the current reality while still achieving our dreams, fostering the children's development, and maintaining our overall health.

The dichotomy of directing while releasing was evident in online homeschooling. We chose to avoid the "great COVID school experiment," as my husband called it, and kept our children home during the first part of the pandemic. Creating safety on one side meant stress on the other. My daughter hated online kindergarten. As a college professor and lover of learning, I cringed every time she emphatically said, "I hate school!" We tried having pep talks, staying positive, and giving rewards. It's not easy to get a kindergartener excited about attending class on a screen. To ease the tension, we decided to set ground rules and let everything else go. To our amazement, she flourished; she learned how to read and excelled at math even though she didn't always pay attention during her online classes or finish every detail of each homework assignment. I realized there was a balance between ensuring she was progressing, without requiring every aspect to be flawlessly completed. In other words, we couldn't let perfection be the enemy of accomplishment.

Another example of balancing my life goals while allowing life to direct me was around expanding our family. The pandemic wasn't an ideal time to have a child, but is there ever an ideal time? There are only so many turns around the sun, and we must make our dreams a reality. Our daughter was born in 2021. The pregnancy was fulfilling and isolating at the same time. Barely anyone knew I was pregnant. We lived our lives in an online world, so close yet so far away from others. We got an intimate view into one another's homes while being physically far apart. It wasn't until spring, when I was outdoors more often, that the growing bump let others know about the baby. Additionally, as a nurse and researcher, I knew the evidence indicated increased risks of adverse outcomes for pregnant women who contracted COVID-19. I also knew vaccines were important, although there was no evidence of how mRNA vaccines would affect a fetus. Balancing the risks and benefits, I learned all I could, emailed experts in the field, and made the decision to get the vaccine. It was another reminder that I can only control so much and have to make decisions with the information available.

In the end, the "great COVID school experiment" sickened my entire family. My daughter brought the virus home from her classroom despite wearing N95 masks, being fully vaccinated, eating lunch in the car, and social distancing. Apparently, I needed to learn once more that I can make plans, but am ultimately not in control. Rolling with what comes my way may not be my natural state, yet I've learned to embrace it and find a balance between holding on and letting go.

Kathryn E. Phillips, PhD, RN. APRN, CHSE
Mother of Lydia (five), Evalyn (four), Henry (six months),*
and Felicity (arrived 2021)
Associate Professor of Nursing
*ages at the onset of the pandemic

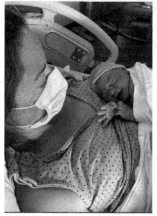

When Failure Is Not an Option

*Take chances, make mistakes, be silly, be imperfect,
trust yourself and follow your heart.*

—*Author unknown*

When I look back on March 2020, I can't believe I survived, but then again, did I have a choice? I was a special education teacher and a single parent to an eight-year-old girl. I was teaching children with varying abilities while navigating new technology, explaining technology to parents, troubleshooting with children remotely, and trying to help my daughter at the same time. I was learning from home and teaching from home; it was an unprecedented time. Throughout this time and even more so now upon reflection, I often thought about one simple question: Is it the personality of a teacher, a mother, or a single mother to just keep going? There is no saying, "No." It was like a version of MacGyver. Just tell me the problem, show me what materials I will have to deal with the problem, and I'm good. There is no "I can't do this." Failure is not an option.

I was like a machine—taking notes on every phone call I made to my students' homes and giving myself five-minute breaks to go to the bathroom and to run upstairs to check on my daughter. While I was teaching downstairs, my daughter was texting me crying emojis from her iPad from upstairs. Every day was a new football game, and I was the coach with a new game plan to address the issues from the day before.

After school hours, I was planning and creating for the next day, and my daughter was crying under the table. She hated learning on the computer, and she just wanted to play with her friends and see people. I knew we were not going back to school for the rest of this school year. I could make it, two and a half months. I could do it. The biggest blow came in the fall of that year when we returned to school. It was decided that teachers would return in person for five days and students would attend every other day. What? I made it through the summer, I survived. I ate my way through bags of Lay's and Lipton Onion Dip. I kept the ship from sinking, but this was too much. I have a daughter who clinically does not do well with change. At first, I thought it was a joke. How could no one have considered that some teachers are parents?

We were frontline workers without being called frontline workers. My daughter who can't handle change was now going to three different caregivers one week and two different caregivers the following week. Yes, you heard that right. She went to school every other day, so there was not really a routine to hold on to for security—not to mention I am a single mom without extra income now paying someone to watch my daughter. When her day to learn from home landed on a Wednesday, I would drive her to my brother's forty-five minutes away—that was a blessing. Who wants to take care of other people's children during a pandemic when they are with other students part of the week? Also, do I want my daughter with other people who may or may not be mask conscious? Who is thinking of and considering us?

The pandemic has provided several important life lessons. I was never strict or overly intense about academics, but during the pandemic and after, I had a new sense of what was most important. Was it important that my daughter got all her work done or that her stress level was not off the charts? Mental health was more than a term; it was a reality in our house. Learning on the computer and doing everything electronically were major stressors, or in my case, they were, at the very least, the straw that broke the camel's back. Not having a lot of our normal human interactions was extremely difficult because it was just the two of us to manage the challenges of any given day. The result? Sometimes I had to just say it's okay, you did enough for today. I was worried that it would set a bad precedent and teach my daughter not to try hard things. But everything about life was hard at that time. Compassion was the most important thing. Thinking outside the box felt mandatory for survival, but it also felt freeing. We drove to Lancaster, PA and bought a puppy, we had picnics on my bed, and had ice cream for dinner! It's okay to do things your own way and make it up as you go along, even when it goes against everything you have done in the past. I gave myself the permission to follow my intuition and focus on what is in my heart and not in my head.

Elissa Cohen
Single mother to Ava (eight)*
Special Educator, Middle School, fifth grade
*age at the onset of the pandemic

When Fear Becomes Reality

*When the thing I feared most happened, it gave me the freedom
to let go of things out of my control. This helped me navigate the
COVID-19 pandemic as a working mom in healthcare.*

—*Jenna Addison*

My health anxiety is worse with my children. Working as a nurse practitioner, I know the reality of things. I know what the best- and worst-case scenarios are, and I play them out in my head. This can be helpful in determining differential diagnosis for your patients. It is not helpful in being anxious about your young kids.

When my youngest started daycare early in 2020, I assumed I would be dealing with a cold or flu for my four-month-old almost immediately. Two days after he started daycare, it happened. He woke up covered in vomit. He had diarrhea that would not stop. I could not even tell if he had urinated. I went to the pediatrician, and she sent us straight to the local children's hospital. This was March 5, 2020. I could hear someone coughing in the ER bay next to us. I brought my own can of Lysol wipes. Of course, we had heard about COVID-19, but we weren't sure how widespread it was. I watched helplessly as an IV was started, and much needed hydration was given to my son. It is my job to help people, and I couldn't help him. Thankfully, although he needed an inpatient stay for electrolyte imbalance from dehydration, he perked up quickly. We left the hospital emotionally and physically exhausted from the ordeal. My health anxiety worries were coming to fruition. If it's possible to be so fatigued from anxiety that nothing touches you, that is where I was.

When days later I was sent home from work because the world was shutting down, I wasn't fazed. I honestly don't remember much from that week, but I do remember my health anxiety was at such a high level from the weeks before that I went numb. I was on autopilot for the next month. Tele-health appointments with a baby on my knee and *Frozen* blaring downstairs for the older toddler was commonplace. I was taking care of other people via Zoom while attempting to take care of myself and my two kids, not knowing what the coming weeks would bring. When we went back into clinic in May 2020, my health anxiety ramped up again but now from a higher baseline. How could I send my children back to daycare? How can a working parent choose between being able to earn a living and compromise safety?

I had to let go of what I could not control, and my kids went back to daycare in the summer of 2020 and absolutely thrived. Despite the little guy getting COVID-19 and several colds and quarantines, they're still thriving. The health anxiety? It's still there. However, there's a perspective that the pandemic placed on all working parents about what is "that bad." For me, "that bad" happened before the world shut down, and we all still got through it. That's it. Getting through it. For a working mom two years into a pandemic with two toddlers, that's enough.

This experience just prior to the stress of the world shutting down gave me an emotional freedom I did not expect. Having anxiety did not prevent my son from getting sick; it didn't add any protection. Health anxiety isn't what helped me parent and work through COVID-19; it's letting go of what you cannot control and knowing that it's okay to just take things day by day. There are things we can do to keep ourselves and our family safe: personal protective equipment (PPE) at work, masks at school, vaccination. But ultimately there is only so much control we have. The best insight this pandemic gave me is shrugging off the unknowns and fears, knowing all I can do is try my best and love my kids. Control what you can. Let the rest go.

Jenna Addison, DNP, FNP-BC, CBCN
Mother of Elizabeth (two) and Eli (five months)*
Breast Surgical Oncology Nurse Practitioner
*ages at the onset of the pandemic

Trust Yourself to Make Hard Decisions

I am not scared. I am compassionate. I am not living in fear.
I am living in a way that proves I want this pandemic to end
and I'm doing what I can to ensure that it does.

—*Rachel Cockrell*

The recent coronavirus pandemic has upended all our lives. My biggest priorities during it were keeping my kids safe and keeping my extended family (my parents and my sisters) safe. To make high quality decisions regarding safe behaviour, it was important to have access to high quality data. I have a PhD in microbiology, so I am fortunate to be able to parse through the scientific information directly from the scientific literature as opposed to typical news sources. I also trusted information published by working mothers who would analyze the data from various studies and share both the validity of the studies and what conclusions could be drawn. With these data in my arsenal, I had to trust that I could make the best decisions for my family to keep us and those around us safe.

At the beginning of the pandemic, there were a lot of unknowns. Initially, we dealt with the lack of information by staying home. Preschools and daycares were closed to combat the spread COVID-19. Schools and businesses were later reopened but with mask wearing, and later vaccines became available. At each progression of the pandemic, as more information became available, I felt it was important for my children to know what was going on, in an age-appropriate way.

Children thrive on predictability and routines, and the pandemic had created a constant flux in our lives. When schools closed or changed to virtual schooling, we explained it was because lots of people were sick, and we had to stay home to be safe until the doctors and scientists could find a way to help. We had to wear masks to school and to the grocery store to keep ourselves safe but also to keep others safe, as sometimes you can get others sick when you don't feel sick yourself. Lastly, we explained to my older son how for our family, it was important for him to get the vaccine, especially since it was not yet available for children like his brother who was under five.

The first two years of the pandemic were isolating and exhausting, especially since we were following social distancing guidelines. This meant that we did not get to see our friends and family as much as we would have liked (or at all, especially the first months). While adhering to the guidelines, we tried to do special things with our kids. Nathan has had two "Zoom birthdays," but gifts were given, the house was decorated, and he had a memorable time. Additionally, we celebrated silly things. We held a party for the four of us when the new *Dog Man* book by Dav Pilkey was released. We made a dessert that looked like one of the main characters, dressed in (customized by me) *Dog Man* t-shirts, and read the book together as a family.

With the information at hand, we made the best decisions we could to keep everyone safe. That said, following the guidelines met with a lot of arguing and resistance with my broader family. This meant that for a small family gathering in December 2020, I insisted upon everyone wearing masks. Likewise in December 2021, I insisted on a negative rapid test before attending. There were family members that protested and those that refused to attend, but I stood my ground. It was disheartening they wouldn't trust me, a PhD scientist, regarding the validity of the pandemic, the virus itself, and/or vaccinations. I am a scientist. Can't they trust me?

As a mother, I realized it was important to trust myself (and science!) to make the best decisions for myself and my family. It is hard to figure out what is trustworthy information, so I try to be patient, kind, and informative to those who ask genuine questions. I believe that everyone wants their children to be happy and healthy, even though our approaches may differ. We are all trying to make the best decisions we can for our loved ones with the highest quality information available at any given time. Ultimately, I had to trust myself when making hard decisions, even if it meant my choices were not the same as others around me.

Catherine Stewart, PhD
Mother of Nathan (two) and Evan (five)*
Senior Scientist, Research Information
*ages at the onset of the pandemic

Working and mothering with the daycare closed at the start of the pandemic.

Trust Children to Do Things

One must trust children to do things.

—Unknown

Growing up in Germany in the 1980s and 1990s, I sometimes heard people say that one should trust children to do things ("man muss Kindern etwas zutrauen"). I understood this to mean that it is good to let children do tasks on their own, even if the tasks might be difficult for them, because it will help them become more independent and confident.

I agreed with this notion, but after I became a mother myself years later (William was born in 2013 and Charlotta in 2015), I often did things for them that they could have done themselves. For example, I helped William with science kits he received for his sixth birthday in December 2019 to the extent that I mostly did the experiments myself, since that was easier and less messy than having him take the lead.

After the children's school in New York City went to fully remote learning in March 2020 due to the COVID-19 pandemic, we spent a few months at my mother-in-law's home in Ridgefield, Connecticut. My husband, Scott, and I both had full-time jobs, and we were grateful that my mother-in-law could help take care of the children while we worked remotely. In September 2020, the children's school began a blended learning schedule, with two in-person days one week and three in-person days the next week. Although Scott and I were in a better position than some other working parents in that we were both able to continue working remotely, the months that followed were still challenging. Our apartment in Brooklyn was small, and on the days the children were doing remote learning, we needed to find a workstation for each of us.

Scott set up his computer in our bedroom, William used a table in the kitchen, and Charlotta and I shared the dining room table. While working in the mornings, I had to also make sure that the children logged on to their online classes and did their assignments. And there was always the feeling that I should be spending more time with them after their classes were done, when I still had to work.

Initially, I tried to keep track of both children's class schedules and make sure they logged on to their online classes while also trying to get some work done in the mornings. However, this resulted in William missing several classes because I got distracted by my work or Charlotta after telling him it was time to log on and he did not log on to his classes without having me nag him. After a few days of this, William and I decided that we would set alerts on our Amazon Echo devices for his class times, and he would be responsible for logging on to his classes without having me remind him. This system worked a lot better, and he rarely missed a class once he took on the responsibility for his own schedule. With Charlotta, I needed to make sure she logged on to her classes, since she really did not like remote learning, but she and I decided that she was responsible for doing her assignments on her own, which she generally did without problems. Giving the children more responsibility not only allowed me to work but also allowed them to avoid my nagging, which seemed to make their classes and assignments more enjoyable for them.

Although I still do too many things for my children, such as helping Charlotta get dressed in the morning even though she is perfectly capable of dressing herself, I try to remind myself that I should trust them to do things on their own. So, when William received a science kit for his birthday last December, I stayed out of his way while he did the experiments by himself. And although there was a mess to clean up afterwards, I am sure it was a better experience for both of us than having me do or micromanage the experiments for him. Overall, I think the challenging times during the pandemic taught us a lot about ourselves and one another and made us a stronger family unit.

Amelie Brewster, Esq.
Mother of William (six) and Charlotta (four)*
Principal Appellate Court Attorney,
New York State Unified Court System
*ages at the onset of the pandemic

No Way of Knowing

My favorite movie has always been the original Gene Wilder version of Ronald Dahl's *Willy Wonka and the Chocolate Factory*. In fact, during the first week of the pandemic shutdown, it made its way onto the color-coded schedule I made for my kids as our Friday night movie. Willy Wonka's lyrics to "The Wondrous Boat Ride" scene had been playing on repeat in my head during the early weeks and months of the pandemic.

My whole existence has hinged on knowing which way I was rowing —become a nurse, become a certified nurse midwife, get married to a really awesome guy, Mike, go back to get a PhD by the age of thirty, have kids (lots of them in my case! Maggie, seven; Isabel, five; Leo, three; and Ethan, nine months), become a tenured and promoted associate professor, make reasonably healthy meals, and keep the kids smiling. Then came a global pandemic with no earthly way of knowing which direction I was going within this unprecedented landscape. With this realization came an exposed vulnerability that I was not accustomed to sharing with the outside world and certainly not with my colleagues. I had spent my years in academia to date with the expected social interactions and answers: Yes, parenting is hard, but I have my mom to help with childcare; yes, four kids are a lot, but my husband, a teacher, is home every day by 3:00 p.m.; and yes, I take on a lot of responsibility, but it's manageable.

There is truth in these statements, but never did I stop and say, "It is a lot. It's heavy. It's hectic. It's pure chaos most days."

These statements are my truths, but they require immense vulnerability. The pandemic for the first time in my thirty-six years of life allowed me the freedom and space to be authentically vulnerable. To admit to colleagues, that this meeting was going to involve me breastfeeding my then nine-month-old son. To admit, I have my camera on for this meeting, but I am still in workout clothes, because the twenty minutes before this meeting was the only time to fit in a workout in my rudimentary home gym. In many ways, it was as if the pandemic had given me permission to be me and to show my life as it really was: messy, happy, busy, loud, and crazy fun. I also truly enjoyed this lens into my colleagues' lives as well. Whether it was learning about their pets, extended family members, partners or kids, the pandemic for me opened up an opportunity for us to be ourselves, to be more vulnerable.

Pre-pandemic, I would have never showed up to teach a class in workout gear; however, when I was home, I let go of any self-judgment and showed up, sometimes still breathless to Zoom meetings or classes, knowing I had prioritized my health and wellness. What I didn't realize until afterwards is that this vulnerability allowed me to quietly show the students that prioritizing my time for self-care in the form of exercise was important. I was silently setting an example of making time for oneself (to my kids as well). In this quiet way, I lead my own version of sharing vulnerability with others—that life can be messy and not always fit into neat boxes, but we can still live it well.

For me, the physical benefits of moving my body will always be secondary to the mental clarity I receive following the rush of endorphins. I can approach my day with more awareness, openness to handle what is coming, and most importantly for me, it allows me to be the mother I want to be for my kids. So almost daily during the pandemic, and afterwards, I hit the ground for push-ups or burpees, often with the kids playing and talking to me. Sometimes my kids abandoned their play and started doing squat jumps behind me. They are perfectly imperfect workouts, but I show up for them for myself and my kids. Living in the perfectly imperfect space of a homemade gym has kept me going, and I don't intend to stop anytime soon. These workouts not only fueled me physically, but more importantly, grounded me in a sense of calm and accomplishment when they were done. This calm then spilled over into every other aspect of my life. I was able to (most days) feel that I was a better mother, partner, and professor for having taken this time to move and experience that rush of endorphins.

What I truly hope for us as working mothers is that the societal expectation of having it all together, leaves for good, and the acceptance of our vulnerabilities remains the acceptable standard for which we begin each meeting and interaction. I am done forever with the fake pleasantries, the image of it all being fine. I don't endorse that we complain and unload at the top of each meeting about every minute detail of our lives, but rather when colleagues ask us how we are, we feel comfortable enough to give the truth, the real answer. I have seen how absolutely freeing this lens that took thirty-six years and a global pandemic to uncover in myself has been. I know my children are watching and listening to all they see and overhear and what a gift I can provide to them so that they know their emotions are not only okay to name but socially acceptable to share. The pandemic made us all vulnerable, emotionally and physically, and as vaccines help us combat the physical vulnerability of severe illness from COVID-19, I know for me, I hope to retain the emotional vulnerability I developed of being a more authentic version of myself: a wife, a daughter, a mother of four, an associate professor, and a certified nurse midwife.

Jenna A. LoGiudice, PhD, CNM, RN, FACNM
Mother of Maggie (seven), Isabel (five), Leo (three),
and Ethan (nine months)*
Associate Professor and Midwifery Program Director,
Egan School of Nursing and Health Studies, Fairfield University
Certified Nurse Midwife, per diem, Greater New Haven OB-GYN
*ages at the onset of the pandemic

Discussion

Compassion for others is a tool of the trade for mothers and a hallmark of the female ethos. Compassion for self, or the ability to extend the same kindness and nonjudgmental understanding toward oneself, is a different story entirely. One of the most prominent pre-pandemic findings in the psychological literature on self-compassion and women is that women excel in providing compassionate care to others but fall significantly short in applying compassion toward themselves (Yarnell et al. 499). This is no surprise given the expectation society places on women to serve all people and things while maintaining a sense of composure and ease. The illusion that such expectations are both normative and doable (insert social media depictions of the happy, balanced, picture-perfect life) leave women perpetually vulnerable to self-criticism, self-doubt, and guilt when they perceive themselves struggling to meet these unrealistic and unsustainable expectations set upon them and socially rewarded by society and the workforce (Maduike 133-35).

The formidable expectation for mothers with both professional careers and children is that they present as poised and put together in a way that makes the nuances of all of her roles nonexistent, with "work" and "home" boxed neatly, separate, and nonintertwining (Poduval and Poduval 63-64). Before the COVID-19 pandemic, family life was expected to stay behind the curtain to provide the center stage for equitable competition and success in the professional world (Maduike 133). These two words needed to be separate and if not under control, then sufficiently and securely managed.

The mothers in this chapter each identify the common experience of having to let go and grow comfortable with appearing as not having it together at all times. They collectively describe granting themselves merciful release from the worry that all women careering and mothering previously shared and were fearful of the world discovering—that we do not always have things in order, under our control, and perfectly balanced. This level of release, in essence, is self-compassion.

Vulnerability became the new, inescapable normal and silent partner in navigating the challenges of mothering, working, schooling, and performing that simultaneously fell upon mothers all at once and without notice. Silent, that is, until not. Longstanding questions—such as "Can we mother and have a professional career?" "Is it wise to allow our professional colleagues access to the 'other side' of us (i.e., the side that is running a household, raising a family, and doing so alongside every work expectation that a man is held to)?" and "Can we permit the public to witness the messiness that is truly our lives despite the appeal to fit in and excel in both circles?"—all came to a sobering head.

Enter the crossover or blending of the worlds that we as mothers with professional careers have always worked so diligently to keep separate; both are now on stage in tandem and openness. It began with the introduction of Zoom and Google Meet. The homes of career women were opened up for colleagues, partners, students, and administrators to see. Even the most polished Zoom background stock image could not protect your meeting, call, or classroom from the untimely interruption of an impatient child, a crying baby, or the appearance of a friendly pet. As Jenna LoGiudice, certified nurse midwife, professor, and mother of four described, the ever-shifting landscape of the pandemic "exposed a vulnerability that I was not accustomed to sharing with the outside world and certainly not with my colleagues." The screen was unveiled. Women working and mothering during the pandemic were inextricably vulnerable.

Our homes, the center of our private lives, became a mecca to all things work, home, play, worship, and fitness. The doors of our homes were opened virtually for the world to see. Advances in visual and audio technology revealed the very messiness that our pre-pandemic selves tried to keep separate and veiled. Anxiety became uniform, and stress was a shared universal. It was now okay to be stressed because the entire world was stressed right along with us; the messiness and imperfections of our daily lives ironically became a source of resilience and connection instead of judgment and isolation.

Finally, the world was able to see the insurmountable toggling act, the sweat, the emotional lability, and the relentless role shifting that mothers who also maintain professional careers need to navigate at all times. As LoGiudice said, "I let go of any self-judgment and showed up, sometimes breathless on Zoom meetings or classes." As per this example, by offering a window into the day and life of LoGiudice, an active mother-professor-midwife allowed for her students to witness the genuine ebb, flow, flux, and rhythm of mothering and careering. This bittersweet reality became sobering and simultaneously self-empowering. A new, free woman was born.

The permission to let go and be vulnerable in our day-to-day coping was liberating for many women, as it also gave them permission to trust their children a little more freely, as Amelie Brewster, a New York City appellate court attorney mother of two noted: "It is good to let children do tasks on their own, even if the tasks are difficult for them.... Giving the children more responsibility not only allowed me to work but also allowed them to avoid my nagging, which seemed to make their classes and assignments more enjoyable for them."

It is in the very handling of our shortcomings and imperfections that we can invite self-compassion to unfold. Kathryn Phillips, a nurse practitioner, an academic, and a pregnant mother with three young children at home, described the tug of this balance between accepting what is and directing your path with an analogy of sand in your hand, reminding us that "If you loosen your fingers or squeeze too hard, the sand will fall." The self-compassionate realization lies in the awareness that the task of maintaining the strands perpetually is unsustainable and that it is okay to embrace, rather than direct to achieve stability.

For Jenna Addison, a breast surgical oncology nurse practitioner and mother to two toddlers, self-compassion meant simply "getting through it," surviving the day: "For a working mother two years into a pandemic with two toddlers, getting through it is enough." Here, self-compassion manifests in the emotional freedom to surrender to the day and meet the demands and inconsistencies of the day to the best degree possible. This insight was further echoed by Elissa Cohen, a special education teacher and single mother to an elementary-school-aged child: "Failure is not an option ... everything about life was hard at that time. Compassion was the most important thing. Thinking outside the box and trying to be normal during a highly abnormal time were thrown out the window for many reasons on many occasions. It's okay to do things your own way and make it up as you go along." In a similar vein, Jenna Addison also asserted: "The best insight this pandemic gave me is shrugging off the unknowns and fears, knowing all I can do is try my best and love my kids. Control what you can. Let the rest go."

Likewise, when Catherine Stuart, a research scientist and microbiologist, was faced with conflicting views from family members about how to best protect her children during a time of uncertainty she asserted, "I had to stand my ground." Thus, even when her views dissented from those whom she loved, and there was a social cost to her extended relationships, she understood that she needed to preserve herself, her integrity, and trust her decision making. Hence, little by little and bit by bit, shavings of self-mercy surfaced.

The narratives in this chapter speak to the crux of self-compassion— that self-compassion diabolically opposes perfectionism by cutting to the common core of all beings, our humanness. Self-compassion embraces that we as a human race across countries and cultures are bathed in vulnerability, imperfection, and fallibility. The stories grouped in this chapter adeptly voice and magnify a shared self-discovery that the pandemic has given us permission to be imperfectly human in front of our colleagues, clients, students, family, and most importantly, ourselves.

By definition, self-compassion includes embracing the following three elements: 1) self-kindness over self-judgment; 2) our common humanity and shared personal experience over isolated existence; and 3) a mindful and a balanced approach to managing negative emotions instead of overidentifying with the negative (Germer and Neff 44; Neff and Germer, "The Transformative Effects"). These stories exemplify this tripartite in spades—the merciful acceptance of our abilities and limits that is not specific to any one being but is shared as a human race.

Steps to Re-imagining

Where can we go from here? The first step is in understanding that self-compassion involves actively recognizing and interrupting critical self-talk with more productive, positive thoughts that aim to enable growth, learning, and healing. In this way, compassion for self begins with the awareness of our internal dialogue (self-talk), which manifests when we perceive that we have erred, fallen short, or lack something expected of us. As astutely relayed by self-compassion scholars Kristin Neff and Christopher Germer, "Self-compassion motivates like a good coach, with kindness, support, and understanding, not harsh criticism" ("Being Kind to Yourself").

Practicing self-compassion regularly, however, is not an easy task. Rather, self-compassion is an act that needs to be cultivated with intention. Thus, self-compassion involves a mindful commitment to monitoring our thought patterns and practicing techniques that allows for us to sit with and nonjudgmentally observe our perceived inadequacies and imperfections (Germer and Neff 43-47). Psychological research has consistently revealed that our brains are neurologically wired to emphasize and cling to the negative, a phenomenon known as "negativity bias" (Vaish et al. 383-84). However, findings also indicate that with intention and exercise we can retrain our brains to hold focus more equitably on the positive (Vaish et al. 383-84). This can be achieved through multiple avenues, including stillness and long kindness meditations, positive self-affirmations, connectedness, and gratitude (Neff and Germer, "Being Kind to Yourself")—themes that will be discussed in the subsequent chapters of this book.

Exercising self-compassion in your work-home life involves a commitment to unlearn a way of thinking that is engrained. This involves steady practice and a committed heart. This chapter affords one small step in creating awareness to change a culture of women generous in their ability to offer compassion to others but starved for it themselves. Let's take this back. Let's take this back, now.

Reflective Prompts

1. Consider two to three ways the pandemic period has forced you to let go of perfectionism and unreal expectations at work. Now consider at least two ways you let go of perfectionism and unreal expectations at home.

2. What did it feel like to be more merciful with yourself and those around you? Recall specific instances and feelings that emerged both at work and home. Did you feel calm? Unrest? Relieved? Or other emotions?

3. How did others at work and home respond to your ability to be more compassionate with yourself?

4. During the current day, where do you tend to be the most perfectionistic? What saying or mantra can you adopt that will remind you to re-imagine compassion for yourself when you find yourself being perfectionistic?

Works Cited

Bricusse, Leslie, and Anthony Newley. "The Wondrous Boat Ride." *Willy Wonka and the Chocolate Factory.* Music from the Original Soundtrack of the Paramount Picture, 1971, CD. Lyrics were modified from the original Ronald Dahl *Charlie and the Chocolate Factory,* New York, Puffin Books, 1964.

Cockrell, Rachel. "I Refuse to Live in Fear is an Excuse for Selfishness." *Scary Mommy Blog,* 24 Nov. 2020, https://www.scarymommy.com/ taking-virus-seriously-not-living-in-fear

Germer, Christopher, and Kristin Neff. "Cultivating Self-Compassion in Trauma Survivors." *Mindfulness-Oriented Interventions for Trauma: Integrating Contemplative Practices,* edited by Victoria M. Follette et al, The Guildford Press, 2015, pp. 43-58.

Maduike, Nneoma. "SFNet Members Roundtable: Effects of the Pandemic on Working Mothers: Asset-Based Financial Services Industry." *The Secured Lender,* vol. 77, no. 4, 2021, pp. 132-141.

Neff, Kristin, and Christopher Germer. "The Transformative Effects of Mindful Self-Compassion." *Mindful,* 29 Jan. 2019, https://www. mindful.org/the-transformative-effects-of-mindful-self-compassion/. Accessed 26 May 2023.

Neff, Kristin, and Christopher Germer. "Being Kind to Yourself: The Science of Self-Compassion." *Compassion: Bridging Theory and Practice: A Multimedia Book,* edited by Tania Singer and Matthias Bolz, Max-Planck Institute, 2013, pp. 291-312.

Poduval, Jayita, and Murali Poduval. "Working Mothers: How Much Working, How Much Mothers, and Where Is the Womanhood?" *Mens Sana Monographs,* vol. 7, no. 1, 2009, pp. 63-79.

Vaish, Amrisha, et al. "Not All Emotions Are Created Equal: The Negativity Bias in Social-Emotional Development." *Psychological Bulletin,* vol. 134, no. 3, 2008, pp. 383-403.

Yarnell, Lisa M., et al. "Meta-Analysis of Gender Differences in Self-Compassion." *Self and Identity,* vol. 14, no. 5, 2015, pp. 499520.

Chapter 4

Grounded in Mindfulness and Faith

Mindfulness isn't difficult, we just need to remember to do it.

—Sharon Salzberg

Groundedness involves firmly routing oneself in the moment and being present without judgment. It allows for inner stability to weather any storm or situation (Stulberg). The ability for each of these women to be fully present in the midst of the pandemic was profound. They were conscious of the weight of the pandemic and all it changed; however, they remained acutely present in all they did in mothering and their career during a tumultuous time. They were each fully present wherever they were. They also found strength in their unwavering faith, trusting confidently in a higher power to guide them through. Furthermore, they embodied gratitude, exemplifying for all those around them, and now for you the reader, the clarity that comes from consciously cultivating a mindset that finds the good, being ever mindful to not take things for granted. The four women in this chapter include a hospitalist clinical educator and frontline healthcare worker; a clinical associate professor and clinically practicing midwife; a licensed psychologist; and an adult probation officer. Three of these mothers have two school-aged children each, and one bravely gave birth to her first child during the outbreak of the pandemic.

"Mama Can't Kiss Us Until She Is Clean. She Saw COVID Today."

The attitude you have as a parent is what your kids will learn from more than what you tell them. They don't remember what you try to teach them. They remember what you are.

—Jim Henson

As if life weren't already enough of a constant hustle as a full-time physician and mother of two, COVID-19 came along and changed our lives in a way none of us had likely ever imagined. As I reflect on the past two years, from the perspective of a frontline healthcare worker, a dubbed "essential employee," I appreciate how this period served as a reset button—a period of much-needed introspection and re-evaluation of how I live and how I wish to mother.

There are moments where I find myself hoping that just like my sur-real memory of childbirth, the experience of these last two years will one day feel like a blur. There are, however, several moments indelibly seared into my memory that relate to my daughter and son (now ages nine and seven, respectively). After all, they were all I could think of as I donned full personal protective equipment for my first COVID-19 pa-tient encounter. I can easily recall the panic and anxiety that set in every time I was notified that I had been exposed to someone who incidentally tested positive for this vicious, unrelenting disease that was holding the world in a vise. Was I putting my family's health at risk? Given my son's underlying asthma, I knew he would be more vulnerable, and my mind would travel to the darkest places, often keeping me awake at night. Initially, I tried social distancing from my family at home, and as any mother with a five-year-old and a seven-year-old will attest, that was not a sustainable option. With time, the kids acclimated to my decontamination routine, as I would arrive home in my blue hospital-issued work scrubs. They would remind one another: "Mama can't kiss us until she is clean. She saw COVID today." These feelings were further compounded by my guilt of not being home to help them navigate the unique challenges involved in distance learning. I would often hear the frustration in their voices: "The other moms are home. Why do you have to go to work all the time?" How could I tell them that I had patients who were fighting for their lives and that they needed me too? With a heavy heart full of mixed emotions, I was highly cognizant of the amplified mommy guilt and the comorbid compassion fatigue that I increasingly faced throughout this time. It is so easy to say, "Why me?" My goal as a parent has always been to raise my children to be independent, self-sufficient adults. I concluded that now was the time to build on their inherent resilience and optimism and fill their toolboxes with the values and beliefs required to confront life's many challenges.

By tapping into my faith, and into the strong roots and values embedded in me by my parents, I found my strength to persevere and lead by example for my children. Despite the chaos the pandemic incited, there was still so much to be grateful for, and we began a new dinnertime tradition of sharing our daily reflections of gratitude.

I focused on being ever present with my children when I was home with them. I shared stories of my day and told them about the patients whom I was able to help and about those whom I could not. To my surprise, not only were they interested to hear about my experience at work, but they also seemed proud of me, too. This provided me with a type of affirmation that I can only describe as distinctly more impactful than any other in my life.

I re-evaluated my life's Venn diagram and realized that I am fortunate to have it be comprised of so many overlapping circles. I realize how delicate, fragile, and unpredictable "it" all is. What a humbling thought that in the big picture, we actually have little to virtually no control of what happens. This was somewhat of a liberating revelation. In my small microcosm, though, I knew I could set a strong example for my children. I chose to find the good in the bad and highlight any silver lining that we could uncover. As things slowly meld into the new normal, I feel truly blessed to continue the working-mom hustle.

Vasiliki Harisis, MD
Mother of Athanasia (seven) and Konstantinos (four)*
Hospitalist Clinician Educator
*ages at the onset of the pandemic

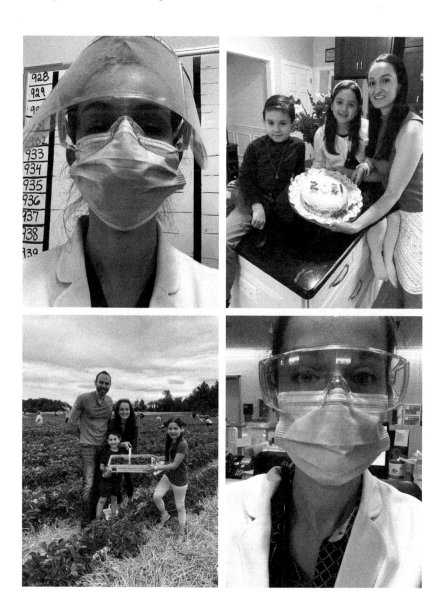

Too Blessed to Be Stressed

I've had many tears and sorrows,
I've had questions for tomorrow,
there's been times I didn't know right from wrong.
But in every situation,
God gave me blessed consolation,
that my trials come to only make me strong.

—Andraé Crouch

"So where are you flying off to now?" "I am going to Jamaica." It's time for the annual family vacation to restore my soul and reground my roots. I am so looking forward to the downtime of just being. Those were my thoughts when we got back from Jamaica in the middle of January 2020. I was so grateful for the time around my family and the beach chair I had claimed as a result of waking up to store odd objects to symbolize "This chair is taken."

My spring semester in the school of nursing started as usual, with expectations being presented at our welcome back to the semester Zoom session. It would have been the first time I was supported in my role as program director. An entire .5 full-time equivalent (FTE) faculty to share my load would finally allow me a moment to breathe. Little did I know that in a few short weeks, things were going to be turned inside out.

As soon as COVID-19 hit the tri-state New York area, I knew my life was forever changed. Was this the end of an era? Being West Indian, any changes in the norm were a sign of the impending end of days. As things progressed and educational facilities started to shut down, I felt confident in the fact that my institution's midwifery program had mastered distance learning for over twenty-five years. As a working mom of two beautiful Jamaican American boys, I have the responsibility to decipher all the changes in the world for them—interchanging the role of mother with the new multifunctional role of friend, entertainer, teacher, personal chef, and protector. I also have a wonderful husband that needs me to be strong, organized, and available for him. Each day I grew weary. However,

Through it all,
through it all,
I've learned to trust in Jesus,
I've learned to trust in God. (Crouch)

I needed to hold on to my faith, for this faith gives me the strength to carry on.

By April, I was emotionally spent. The only thing that was giving me a moment of peace was my at least thirty minutes of mindfulness. Mindful moments included yoga in my in-house studio, outside walking, or riding my newly purchased ProForm bike. Most of my students were not completing clinical hours, and two Zoom meetings a day had now turned into six to seven hours of virtual meetings.

Am I tired or am I weary? Do these kids know that cooking three hot meals and snacks is a luxury? I am happy to do it for them. I am happy to see them grow and to protect them and keep them safe. But to be honest, can y'all stop talking, humming, and making noise? I need a minute to think. Are they really using all their electronic devices to do schoolwork and play computer games? I wonder if they know having a desktop, iPad, and a chrome book is a luxury?

I've been to lots of places,
I've seen a lot of faces,
There's been times I felt so all alone.
But in my lonely hours,
yes, those precious lonely hours,
Jesus lets me know that I was His own. (Crouch)

Can the two of you stop arguing? I have a Zoom meeting now. Please Lord.... I will scream if someone asks if we can hear them or see their screen?

Through it all,
through it all,
I've learned to trust in Jesus,
I've learned to trust in God.
Through it all,
through it all,
I've learned to depend upon His Word. (Crouch)

I've also learned that drinking Jamaican white rum does not help clean COVID-19 out of your throat.

The most important lessons learned will never be unlearned. These were lessons in compassion, love, and patience. We learned that "I can't breathe" will always be taken seriously. This time spent at home with the boys taught them how to feel, communicate those feelings, and be seen in this world. They were empowered, loved, and this empowerment gave birth to a new energy in me to continue on. I am grateful for them. They helped heal my confused weary heart because love for them is simple and kind.

I thank God for the mountains,
and I thank Him for the valleys,
I thank Him for the storms He brought me through.
For if I'd never had a problem,
I wouldn't know God could solve them,
I'd never know what faith in God could do. (Crouch)

Through it all... I got through it all.

Heather Findletar Hines, DNP, CNM, FACNM
Mother of James (ten) and William (seven)*
Clinical Associate Professor, Midwifery Program Director,
and Clinical Midwife
*ages at the onset of the pandemic

Jan 18, 2020 –
fresh from vacation

April 3, 2020
– keeping arts
and crafts going

Teaching and
practicing yoga
from my basement
studio.

The Unexpected Joys of
the Pandemic

Enjoy the little things in life because one day you'll
look back and realize they were the big things.

—*Kurt Vonnegut*

On March 16, 2020, at the beginning of the pandemic in the
Northeast region of the US, my entire office was sent home due
to my friend and coworker testing positive for COVID-19. We
were the first probation office in our state to have a positive case and
be sent home. As a mother, I suddenly found myself home with two
elementary-school-aged children, helping them navigate through the
world of virtual learning. As a probation officer with a specialized caseload of high-risk women offenders with trauma, I suddenly found myself
home without any access to my cases and completely detached from the
women that I serve. As a hazardous duty officer, I had no access to my
files, records, and any mechanism that would allow me to work from
home hazardous duty professionals are never eligible to work from home.
I worried for these women daily despite trying to focus on helping my
children do their work and coping with the sudden detachment from their
extended family, friends, and social life. My clients are mothers living in
homeless shelters, mothers in abusive relationships, single mothers out
of work, and mothers who struggle with addiction. I had no way of con-
tacting them and helping them navigate through the pandemic as I do in
their day-to-day life. I struggled with this feeling of powerlessness for
weeks; I felt torn between my family life and worry for them. I just prayed
that they would be okay as I prayed that my family would be, too.

After a few weeks away from work, I found myself more at ease and focussed on being in the present, worrying less, and being thankful that my family was healthy and safe. Despite the uncertainty of what was going on at the time, I found great joy in having the opportunity to be home with my children. Working fulltime is always a juggling act between rushing in the morning and spending a few precious hours with them in the evening while taking them to and from activities, making dinner, and helping them with their homework. Social events, soccer games, dance class, and family time were crammed in two short days on the weekend. Lastly, we would have to wait the whole year for a week of vacation where we could spend time as a family. The pandemic made me a stay-at-home mother for two months, and I honestly enjoyed every second. I enjoyed taking long walks with them, talking to them, laughing with them, as well as having dance parties and movie nights with them. I would sometimes dream about being a stay-at-home mother, but I also loved my career and could not see myself actually ever giving it up. This was my opportunity, and I thanked God for giving me the chance to spend so much quality time with my children who are growing up so fast.

After two months of being home, I was able to return to work two days a week. I checked in on my clients, and they were all doing well and managing as best as they could. They found their own silver lining in this pandemic, and being the self-sufficient women that they were, they were able to push through and get by. They were just as happy to hear from me as I was to hear from them, and they were equally as concerned for my wellbeing as I was for theirs. Although I was their probation officer and held a role of authority over them, we felt a sense of comradery and just talked like women who had gone through a pandemic. Together, we were grateful that the other had gotten through the worst part.

As time went on, I went into the office more and also received a phone and laptop to be able to work from home on the remaining days. For the next year, I worked on a hybrid schedule, which managed to be on the same one as my children. This by far was the dream. I was home with them on their remote days and at the office when they were in school. Although I loved being home with my kids, I was happy to be back in the office with my coworkers and doing the work I love. It also gave me time to myself to be social and have a break from mommy duties.

This past year and a half gave me insight into several things. As a mother, I thought about how important it is to just be present, how important time with your loved ones is, and how this in itself is the greatest gift. The beauty in slowing things down and not rushing and not having to fill your days with events. Our children don't need as much as we think they do, the most important thing is our time, love, and compassion. As a working mother, I became aware of how important it is to have balance. Being able to separate from my children and focus on myself is important to my wellbeing. Catching up with friends, having lunch dates, going shopping and doing things for me fuel me. As a probation officer I was reminded that I and the women I supervise are similar in many ways. Although our unique circumstances have put us in different paths in life, we are all women trying our best to get through the struggles and challenges that are brought our way. As mothers, we do our best with what we have to do right by our children. At this time of our lives, we were all going through the same pandemic and the same fear. This was the most humbling experience of all.

I hope as we break free from this pandemic, I continue to remember these life lessons and continue to savour the simple joys in life.

Yianna Dimitroglou, MA
*Mother of a nine-year-old girl and six-year-old boy**
Adult Probation Officer, State of Connecticut Judicial Branch
*ages at the onset of the pandemic

Wow! That Was One Frightening Experience

When troubles of any kind come your way, consider it an opportunity for great joy. For you know that when your faith is tested, your endurance has a chance to grow. So let it grow, for when your endurance is fully developed, you will be perfect and complete, needing nothing.

—Holy Bible, James 1:2-4

After receiving the amazing news that I was finally pregnant after years of miscarriages, I was beyond thrilled. My pregnancy was consumed with so many cautionary yet praise-filled feelings. It was an emotional roller coaster (to say the least) for the duration of my entire pregnancy. I thought being told by my medical team that I needed to go on bed rest, as a result of my high-risk pregnancy, for two months prior to my due date (April 2020) would be the most challenging part I needed to endure. I was clearly wrong and in store for a rude awakening.

Shortly after going on bed rest, the world as we knew it shut down, literally, as a result of the COVID-19 global pandemic. Everything changed in an instant. The manner in which I visited my doctors who were closely monitoring my pregnancy changed; the protocols were continuously changing on a daily basis, and my anxiety (which I never experienced before) was at high. Due to my delivery date being in April 2020, which was at the height of the pandemic, and in accordance with my state's (New York) guidelines at the time, my husband was not allowed to stay in the hospital with me during the time I was there recovering from a caesarean section. He was only allowed to be with me during the delivery (and only if he tested negative) but then had to exit the hospital promptly two hours after I gave birth. What?!?! I struggled for years to have a child, and I would have to now endure the most frightening yet beautiful experience of a lifetime alone.

After giving birth (while wearing a mask), the doctors allowed me to hold my precious miracle baby, and all I could do was cry tears of joy. The experience of holding my daughter for the first time while wearing a mask was so disturbing and created a barrier for me to kiss her and allow our faces to touch to have that incredibly vital initial contact. Once I was taken to my hospital room alone, I was flooded with emotions; being frightened and terrified were definitely at the top of that list! The hospital staff was amazing, but they too were protecting themselves as they cared for my baby and me; they wore masks, gloves, and protective gowns. I was told I couldn't leave my room due to COVID-19 protocols, and my baby would be brought back and forth to me from the nursery. Every part of my hospital experience was unimaginably daunting and cannot be articulately described.

After being released from the hospital, the frightening journey continued. I faced the challenges of recovering from a cesarean birth at home, relatively alone, because family and friends could not visit the house to help due to concerns of potentially exposing my baby or myself to COVID-19 and the potential detrimental effects of that. This reality was coupled with being a new mom and not really knowing what to do to care for my baby. Close family members did whatever way they could to help, but they always wore a mask around myself and the baby; even my husband wore a mask, as he was exercising an abundance of caution. Having a baby is a miracle in itself, but never in my wildest imagination did I ever fathom my childbirth experience would be what it was.

During that time, my faith was tested beyond my level of comprehension. It was challenging in that moment to consider it an opportunity for great joy. Now that my daughter is twenty-one months and thriving, I can only now reflect on the insights that have emerged from that time. I believe that I have always been a woman who was tenacious, determined, and confident. However, through this experience, I believe that more so than ever. The insight that emerged is that I can do all things through Christ Who strengthens me, and as long as I unwaveringly trust in Him and His Will for my life, all will be well. I am one who flourishes in leadership positions, and oftentimes, I feel the need to be in control of my circumstances to whatever extent possible. The experience of pregnancy and childbirth during a global pandemic has reminded me in a very vivid, surreal way that God has been, is, and will always be in control. Releasing my anxieties allows me to rest in His perfect peace!

This insight has changed me and definitely shaped how I will re-imagine how I will work and be a mother as a result. In regard to my work as a psychologist, I am already in a helping profession; however, I am learning to practice more mindfulness and to be fully present in the moment so that each experience is meaningful, and I am intentional about making it count. I am also making efforts to help support the students and families I work with to also engage in more mindfulness experiences to help them manage their anxieties as well as feel more empowered to be in control of the gift of the present moment. I carry this mindfulness over to my mothering as well and make every attempt to truly savor each and every moment with my daughter while blocking out the noise of all of those things (and people) that can be quantified as distractions. These are opportunities of great joy because my endurance is growing and continuously refining me into a more perfect version of who God created me to be.

Dr. Nikimya Ligon , MAT, MS.Ed, CAS, Psy.D.
Mother of Mia Barnes (arrived April 2020)
NYS Licensed Psychologist/CT Certified School Psychologist

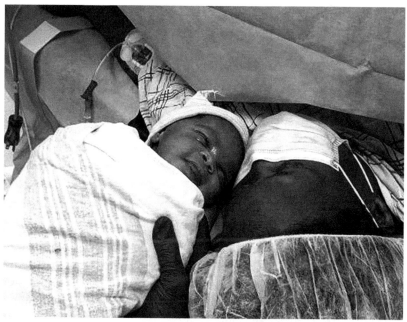

Discussion

"Mindfulness" is a word that gained traction during the pandemic. For those who practice mindfulness, this routine was a pandemic lifeline. For others, their deep-rooted faith saw them through. Importantly, intentionally holding space for mindfulness and leaning on their faith provided moments of clarity and focus for many working mothers during the pandemic.

Being mindful doesn't tell you how to think; rather, it gives you permission to sit with how you are thinking and feeling right here, right now (Penman). Mindfulness is not how you were feeling a few hours ago or your worry about something that might happen in the morning; instead, it involves the commitment to reflect and be present in exactly where you are right in the current moment—to honor all the feelings you are having and just intentionally be with those feelings. Mindfulness involves not only being aware of your thoughts and cognitions but focussing on your entire physical body as well and how it feels in that moment. When being mindful, you use all of your senses.

One of the most recognizable mindfulness exercises is depicted in this image of walking with a child (Forbes Öste). The following few steps will help incorporate the practice of being truly mindful and releasing your full mind. First, press your feet into the ground, and you will feel a connectedness to the earth. Next, turn to your senses of smell and hearing. Do you smell rain? Do you smell gas from cars driving past or freshly cut grass? Do you hear birds chirping, sirens, church bells? Or is it simply the wind rustling the leaves or cars driving by? Next, focus on all that you see in your surroundings. Notice everything around you intentionally as if someone were going to ask you to share as much detail as possible with them later. If you are walking alongside someone, what does it feel like to hold their hand, to be in their company, to give them your undivided attention? What is it like to release your full mind and just see the path ahead and the person you are with?

Mind Full, or Mindful?

@forbesoste

We have all been in the place where our minds are full—full of toxic worry about yesterday and tomorrow, wondering if we said the right things in a meeting, or if the chicken will be defrosted in time for dinner. The list is maddeningly endless. Being mindful, in contrast, is grounding oneself like the child in this image—exactly where you are, right now in this current moment and space. Being truly present is that simple; however, it takes practice and patience to cultivate it in oneself. We are used to always running and worrying about the next work meeting and then the next event for our kids, and during the pandemic, this meant so clearly having to know exactly what time and what zoom link to use, adding more stress and more layers. When we aim to be mindful, we are in the moment fully. We are allowing ourselves to be here now. Being present allows for us to work efficiently, but more importantly, it allows for us to show up and enjoy the beautiful chaos that is motherhood (Crockett and Roy). Mindfulness doesn't require everything to go well; in fact, it calls on us most in times of turmoil. It asks us to focus on where we are in that moment and to sit with that exact moment in time. We can be here now as these mothers so poignantly show us in their stories.

Being mindful is inherent to motherhood as we know that our kids will remember most not the things we tell them, but rather how they see us cope and move through this world, navigating both the mundane and the heavy parts of life (Cogner; Crockett and Roy). As Heather, a professor and midwife, reflects: "As a working mom of two beautiful Jamaican American boys, I have the responsibility to decipher all the changes in the world for them." To do so, she leaned into her faith deeply to garner the strength to carry on. And when weariness and emotional exhaustion showed up much like an uninvited dinner guest, practicing mindfulness daily, along with her faith, saw her through. Her insights were a culmination of all of these forces: "The most important lessons learned will never be unlearned. These were lessons in compassion, love, and patience. We learned that 'I can't breathe' will always be taken seriously. This time spent at home with the boys taught them how to feel, communicate those feelings, and be seen in this world."

Similarly, Vasiliki, a hospital doctor and mother of two, discusses how being ever present with her children was her one sure anchor through the pandemic. She was bravely working on the frontlines, a local healthcare hero, but more important than that title, for her children, she was the leading superwoman of their home. Day in and day out, as the pandemic raged, she cared for COVID-19–positive patients, and she intentionally spoke about her work, not hiding the harsh realities of the illness from her children. Instead, they acutely learned from her: "Mama can't kiss us until she is clean. She saw COVID today." She was mindful to balance the fact that her career as a medical doctor took her outside of her home, pandemic or not. This was the trade-off for her and all frontline workers—facing a brutal honest reality but then arriving home to a sanctuary of love and togetherness. Her kids' reality was that the vast majority of their peers now had their own mothers at home, but they did not. How did she rise to the occasion and assuage the mom guilt she so poignantly details experiencing? She was mindful and intentional. She seized the opportunity to boldly foster resilience in her children. She filled their life toolboxes with lessons about her steadfast and unwavering commitment to being a healthcare provider during the pandemic. She pulled on her strong faith to see her way through. She was ever mindful and intentional to introduce a new dinner-time tradition with her children of sharing their daily reflections of gratitude with one another. She demonstrated to her children exactly what a hero is and does through her daily presence as both a mother and a frontline doctor.

It is so easy to despair in times of extensive turmoil. Consciously working on mindful presence and appreciation does not ignore all the negativity in the world, as Vasiliki and Heather have shown us; rather, it purposely allows us to reframe the dichotomy of challenge and blessings. Finding one's center in the present, in gratitude, or in faith reminds us what is rather than what is not. Yianna, an adult probation officer and mother of two, found that prayer saw her through the feelings of powerlessness the pandemic brought. She prayed for her family and her caseload of high-risk women, who were survivors of trauma. She became present and found great joy in being home with her children. When the lockdown ended, and she could resume in-person work with her clients, she found a common denominator: They too had found moments of joy. Together, they all spoke of gratitude for surviving the shutdown. There was a shared comradery threaded together by the connecting tentacles of motherhood between them all—a moment she did not take for granted. She was mindful of the following: "Although our unique circumstances have put us on different paths in life, we are all women trying our best to get through the struggles and challenges that are brought our way. As mothers, we do our best with what we have to do right by our children."

Notably, prayer is a form of mindfulness, as it allows quiet space for the mind to be present with the words they are praying in that moment and to call on a higher power for strength. As was seen in these narratives, faith and religiosity were a pillar for these women during the pandemic. Research on adaptive coping during the pandemic has found that positivity, spirituality, faith, trust in God, scripture, and prayer have all played a significant role in women's ability to cope with the stress of the pandemic, served as buffers and protection from anxiety, and allowed for hope for the future (Javeed and Parveen 4-5; June and June 184-85; Roberto, et al. 1326; Sweeney et al. 744).

Nikimya, a psychologist who gave birth to her first child during the pandemic near New York City, offers that although her faith was tested beyond comprehension, God released her anxieties and allowed her to be present through the daunting experiences that was giving birth during the pandemic: "God has been, is, and will always be in control." She learned to re-imagine how she works and how she mothers. She learned to practice more mindfulness and be intentional about making it count. In her work, she has taken her insights from birthing and mothering during the pandemic and now shares them with others. She tries to help support the students and families with whom she works to also engage in more mindfulness experiences to help them manage their anxieties and feel more empowered.

Mindful mothering was present throughout these women's narratives (Cogner; Crockett and Roy). Each mother illustrated a deep appreciation for the intricacies, the pain, the joys, the triumphs, and the tribulations that motherhood brings with it. The women whose insights and awakenings you just read embodied mindful mothering by intentionally rising to the moment and leading by example to show their children how to be, how to breathe, and how to work toward resiliency in times of deep uncertainty. As Nikimya explains: "I carry this mindfulness over to my mothering as well and make every attempt to truly savor each and every moment with my daughter while blocking out the noise of all of those things (and people) that can be quantified as distractions."

We can learn from these women how to more intentionally embrace mindfulness and its benefits. As Vasiliki reflects: "I re-evaluated my life's Venn diagram, and realized I am fortunate to have it comprised of so many overlapping circles. I appreciate how this period served as a reset button—a period of much-needed introspection and re-evaluation of how I live and how I wish to mother." Research during the pandemic on working mothers in India also found that mindfulness was also a part of the pandemic experience (Mazumdar and Gupta 476; Mazumdar et al. 6): "A woman's mindful approach toward herself and parenting [during the pandemic] allowed for identification of her values and purpose in life, which made her appreciate her growth and further contributed to an overall sense of meaning in life" (Mazumdar et al. 6). Importantly, we too must work to accept where we are right now and sink into the moment, firmly grounding ourselves in it. We can then be fully present and remember that patience and vulnerability are also necessary for mindfulness (Stulberg)—traits you have just read and learned more about in the previous chapter on compassion for self.

Steps to Re-imagining

Finding the good in one's surroundings and being grounded were possible for these mothers through mindfulness, meditation, prayer, and faith. They each demonstrate how using the quiet space of prayer and meditation provided peace and a sense of appreciation during the pandemic, allowing them to navigate their way through the pandemic in all of their roles. Intentionally sinking into the moment, grounding, and centering themselves in gratitude helped to remind them of what is rather than what is not. Just as these mindful mothers exemplify, mindfulness starts with leaning deeply into the present and allowing yourself to simply be here now and to see, feel, taste, hear, and smell without judgment. We ask you to remind yourself to be here now in the many facets of your life.

Reflective Prompts

1. Describe a time when you were mindful and how that helped you.

2. Are you rooted in this moment through mindfulness? Are you using all of your senses to be aware, without judgment, of what you see, feel, taste, hear, and smell? Right now, we offer to you to sink into this moment and use all of your senses to be intentionally present in this exact moment.

3. Can you make a commitment to intentionally be mindful the next time you get into your car, make dinner, or go for a walk? (These are all places where we often find ourselves but don't show up mindfully.) How specifically will you remind yourself to be mindful in these moments? Write down your plan and then place a note somewhere you will see it with the words: "Be Mindful."

4. How does prayer (or quiet reflection) play a role in your life and how does it serve you?

Works Cited

Cogner, Dannielle. "Mindful Mothering: The Art of Being Present." *Sandra Dodd*, 2005, https://sandradodd.com/mindfulness/danielle.

Accessed 29 May 2023.

Crouch, Andrea. "Through It All." *LyricsMania*, https://www.lyricsmania.com/through_it_all_lyrics_andrae_crouch.html. Accessed 29 May 2023.

Crockett, Molly, and Sandip Roy. "The Mindful Mother: Practicing Mindfulness in Motherhood." *The Happiness Blog*, https://happyproject.in/mindful-mother/. Accessed 29 May 2023.

Forbes Öste, Heidi. Image: "Mind Full v. Mindful." Flickr. https://www.flickr.com/photos/forbesoste/15655214702 Accessed 12, July 2022.

Henson, Jim. *It's Not Easy Being Green: And Other Things to Consider.* Peter Pauper Press, Inc., 2007.

Holy Bible. New Living Translation. Tyndale House, 2006.

Javed, Sarah, and Heena Parveen. "Adaptive Coping Strategies Used by People during Coronavirus." *Journal of Education and Health Promotion*, vol. 10, no. 122, 31 Mar. 2021, doi:10.4103/jehp.jehp_522_20

June, Lee N., and Shirley A. June. "Initial Real Time Coping by African American Christians during the Coronavirus Pandemic (COVID-19)." *Journal of Pastoral Care & Counseling*, vol. 75, no. 3, 2021, pp. 179-87.

Mazumdar, Ketoki, and Pooja Gupta. "The Invisible Frontline Workers: Narratives of Indian Mothers' Experiences through the Pandemic." *Mothers, Mothering, and COVID-19: Dispatches from the Pandemic*, edited by Andrea O'Reilly and Fiona Joy Green, Demeter Press, 2021, pp. 467-78.

Mazumdar, Ketoki, et al. "Vignettes of Mothering through the Pandemic: A Gendered Perspective of Challenges and Making Meaning of Motherhood in India." *Women's Studies International Forum*, vol. 90, 2022, pp. 1-7.

Penman, Danny. "What Exactly Is Mindfulness? It's Not What You Think." *Psychology Today*, 19 June 2018, https://www.psychologytoday.com/us/blog/mindfulness-in-frantic-world/201801/what-exactly-is-mindfulness-it-s-not-what-you-think. Accessed 29 May 2023.

Roberto, Anka, et al. "Impact of Spirituality on Resilience and Coping during the COVID-19 Crisis: A Mixed-Method Approach Investigating the Impact on Women." *Health Care for Women International*, vol. 41, no. 11-12, 2020, pp. 1313-34.

Salzberg, Sharon. "Mindfulness Isn't Difficult, We Just Need to Remember to Do It." *Twitter*, 24 July 2021, https://mobile.twitter.com/SharonSalzberg. Accessed 29 May 2023.

Stulberg, Brad. "Why Groundedness Is the New Key to Success" *Forbes*, 13 Sept. 2021, https://www.forbes.com/sites/melodywilding/2021/09/13/why-groundedness-is-the-new-key-to-success/. Accessed 29 May 2023.

Sweeney, Allison M., et al. "Evaluating Experiences of Stress and Coping Among African American Women During the COVID-19 Pandemic to Inform Future Interventions." *Health Education & Behavior*, vol. 48, no. 6, Dec. 2021, pp. 739-46.

@Kurt_Vonnegut (Kurt Vonnegut). "Enjoy the little things in life..." *Twitter*, 8 June 2012, https://twitter.com/Kurt_Vonnegut/status/244556876447096833. Accessed 13 June 2023.

Chapter 5

Choosing Gratitude

It's the first time I see that we have a choice: to pay attention
to what we've lost or to pay attention to what we still have.

—*Edith Eger 38*

It can often seem there is no brightness on a stormy day, but then the clouds part, allowing a ray of light to shine through, which reminds us that there is goodness amid the clouds. The pandemic was an unexpected and unwelcome change; it intensely struck mothers and threw their world into disarray. In this unsettling time, the four women in this section all chose to take a fresh look at their drastically altered daily existence of working and schooling from home and chose to adjust their focus and actively scan their environments to find the good amid the bad—the light amid the darkness. Their insights remind us that we all have the power to decide how we will view a situation. You will hear from a small business owner, a corporate executive, a teacher, and an account-ant, all with young children ranging in age from two to eight at the onset of the pandemic. Each of these women describes how they consciously chose to find the gifts in their lives during the arduous days of the pandemic.

Why "Pandemic Mom" Is a Job Title

*Acknowledging the good that you already have in
your life is the foundation for all abundance.*

—*Eckhart Tolle*

The pandemic has been hard. Really hard. As a working mom, I get PTSD just thinking of our time in quarantine. Having to manage through homeschooling, cooking, cleaning, and my work left me little time for personal care both mentally and physically. But there is always a silver lining to a dark cloud, and I felt that I gained a lot of insight into what I need as a woman and mother to be happy. There were many lessons that were learned during this time that changed not only the way I mother but also how I manage my life and personal time.

The first lesson I came to grips with quickly was that I had to let go of my constant need to keep everything organized and orderly at home. The house was going to be a mess at times. Having food wrappers, coloring paper, markers, and random toys all over the place doesn't mean I am messy. It means our home is being lived in, and we are doing things. And that is okay. Before the pandemic, we barely had time to spend at home, as we were rushing to and from school, work, sports, after-school activities, and playdates. We were always on the go. Initially, I was getting so aggravated with the chaos. Once I let that go and accepted the chaos, I was much more relaxed and happier. We would schedule certain times that would be cleanup sessions, but in between, I would let go of my constant need for order because at the end of the day, it really wasn't that important. I realized it was more important to do fun things and bond as a family.

That brings me to my next point. I realized how important and special our family time is. Don't get me wrong. I knew it was important before, but never in my life had I been home with family for this long of a time. I realized how much noise I let into my life before COVID-19. I was pulled in way too many directions and didn't fully appreciate the special time I did have with my family. I was constantly thinking about what was coming up next versus focusing on the present. I have learned to say "no" now. I am more selective with what takes me away from them, and I cherish the down time I have at home. There were many things that filled my days and weeks that weren't really fulfilling, but I was doing them anyways. I now need to feel like I am getting something positive out of everything I do for it to be worth sacrificing my family time. Basically, I have slowed the pace of my life, and as a result, I have felt more at peace with myself. I am more present as a mother, and it's deepened the relationship I have with my son. I have the time to pick him up from school most days, work on homework together, play games, and just be silly. I look back on how frantic I was in the time before COVID-19, and I can never picture myself going back to that level of intensity ever again.

Beyond just my own self, I realized how much I loved and appreciated others. Just being able to hug my mom or see my son play with my dad was taken away from us, leaving huge gaping holes in our hearts. Our heightened dependency on technology to stay in touch became a critical part of our everyday life. We made it a point to have regular facetime calls and see each other, even if it was virtual. It heightened our appreciation and love for one another and even now, a year later, just seeing family in person is even more special for us all.

I had always assumed that to have this level of calm, it would come at the expense of my career. It couldn't be further from the truth. I now am more productive than ever during the hours I am working. I know that by doing this, I will feel more relaxed when I turn off. It's made me a better coworker and employer as I now take the time to listen more than ever before and can control my emotions easier. I take everything into perspective now. I think about how at the height of COVID-19, I was concerned about our lives and how everything else seemed so insignificant. Reflecting on that memory helps me to stay level headed and not get bothered anymore by small annoyances.

All in all, the lessons I have incorporated into my life now have all been positive and additive to my personal wellbeing. Although it took a global pandemic to get me to come to this realization, I am still thankful for the way it changed my life into one where I am more appreciative, present, relaxed, and hyperaware of what really matters.

Irina Kapetanakis
Mother of Lucio (six)*
Owner of Rumble Hoboken, Chief Experience Officer at Corben & Lane
*age at the onset of the pandemic

No Longer Running

The days are long, but the years are short.

—Gretchen Rubin

Since becoming a mother, the saying "The days are long, but the years are short" has never meant more. Pre-pandemic life would entail me waking up at 5:00 a.m., getting ready for work to be on the road by 6:00 a.m., sitting in traffic for an hour, and then arriving at the office for 7:00 a.m. I would bounce around from meeting room to meeting room (and when the babies were infants, I would pump in between or during meetings). I would then start to look out my window at 4:00 p.m. and get anxious about the traffic in hopes I would be able to pick up my kids on time at 5:00 p.m. from daycare. We would then get home, eat dinner, go to bed, and repeat it all the next day. I felt my life was a constant rush, yet it was also filled with regret. I wish I could have stayed home with my kids, but I knew both financially and mentally that it was just not in the cards for me. I enjoy the mental rush of work and the added purpose it brings to my life.

Fast forward to March 2020, and COVID-19 forced my whole office to work from home. Yes, I still had my meetings (some were with kids hanging all over me), but I no longer had to run from meeting room to meeting room on opposite sides of buildings or floors and did not have to worry at all about traffic. It was simply amazing. I felt grateful. I was able to see my kids for breakfast, lunch, and dinner. I could see them between meetings or even during my calls. For once in my life, I felt I could have both—be a mother and have a career.

The pandemic has helped speed up the necessary change in the business world. It made everyone more real. We all suddenly knew one another's kids, families, and even dogs. We all knew we had to get our jobs done, but we could do it on our own time. Before the pandemic, as a working mother, I would feel guilty wanting to leave work to go to one of my kid's events or having to stay home with a sick kid and wondering if my boss was judging the fact that I was staying home and not my husband. There was an added stress balancing it all: When I was at work, I wanted to be home, and when I was home, I wanted to be at work. Now the business culture has evolved, and we can work from home, without judgment. This situation was forced upon us with COVID-19, but it has shown businesses that it does work and has given mothers like me the opportunity to no longer feel that regret or longing to be somewhere else.

Every day I look at my kids and cannot believe how quickly they are growing up. Now my oldest is in kindergarten, and I wonder where the time has gone. I'm thankful I can walk her to the bus stop each morning and be there to greet her each afternoon, which would have never been an option before the pandemic. I can leisurely leave my house ten minutes before 5:00 p.m. to make sure I get my other daughter from daycare on time. I still spend plenty of early mornings and late nights working, but being able to see my kids when I want has made all the difference because "The days are long, but the years are short." And I want to be there for it all.

Stephanie Drew, CPA, MSA
Mother of Abigail (four) and Madison (just turned two)*
Controller
*ages at the onset of the pandemic

Maintaining an Emotionally Healthy Child during the Pandemic

Live everyday as if it's your last.

— Unknown

This quote more than any has resonated with me the most throughout this pandemic. March 13, 2020, will forever be burned in my memory. I was working in our family barbershop and heard on the news that a virus was spreading rapidly overseas and also in the United States (US). From the report on the news, I realized that I may be an easy target, as many of my clients travel abroad regularly for work and sometimes pleasure.

That day, I left in the middle of work and immediately went to the supermarket and bought enough food to last for approximately two weeks. I had also decided to close the shop for two weeks in order to protect myself and my family from catching this awful virus. Three days later, as more information came about on this virus, the Health Department sent all the local businesses a notification that we all needed to shut down business for a month. The Friday before that happened, my daughter's school also sent home a notice that there would be no in-person classes indefinitely. That began my journey of parenting through the scariest time of my life—the COVID-19 pandemic.

Over the next few days and weeks, my wife and I monitored the situation closely. My daughter was sent home with instructions on how to log on to her computer daily to continue her schoolwork. In the beginning, I was happy to have a few days off to be home with her. I was able to provide her the space and structure to do her work. We got up as usual, got dressed, ate breakfast, and logged on to school, but after three weeks of this, she didn't want to be in her room alone anymore, and doing schoolwork also became a hassle. I have to admit that it was also becoming tougher on me to teach her half the day and then attend to all my other responsibilities.

I soon realized that this wasn't a two-week or month-long situation, and my therapeutic training kicked in to get us through this. Having an undergraduate degree in psychology and masters in social work came in handy during this time. I knew the mental impact this situation could create for both of us if we didn't acknowledge and address how drastically things had changed in our lives. I relied heavily on my training and experience to tackle some of the emotions we were dealing with daily. I could see that the COVID-19 situation was causing my daughter some anxiety, and I had to try my best to alleviate as much of it for her as I possibly could while also dealing with my own.

As we were updated on the infection and death rates, I realized that I was becoming comfortable with just staying in the house and watching television, cooking and cleaning, and avoiding everyone, but I had a seven-year-old who needed her environment to be as stable and normal as possible. On any given day, parenting isn't the easiest job, but throw a pandemic in the mix, and I knew that I had to do everything in my power to shield her from the ugliness of this virus. I also knew that I also had to educate her on COVID-19 as much as a seven-year-old could comprehend, since it was impacting her daily life, too. It became very clear to me that life, especially now, was too short and we had to live each day to the fullest.

As difficult as it was for me to take on the daily chores, teach her, and figure out how my partner and I were going to protect our business, I had to make time to get her outside so that she could ride her bike and play with the neighborhood kids from a distance. In doing that, I too saw a difference in my mood. Facebook Kids Messenger saved the day by giving her the ability to see and interact with her friends during the day. During this time, I adjusted her screen time daily depending on what I needed to get done that day. As long as she was interacting with her friends and laughing and playing Roblox, I was okay with that.

Some days, I had to focus on getting the shop ready to reopen, which meant I was away from home for a few hours. Other days, we spent a lot of time outdoors walking or riding our bikes. Other days, we watched movies, played games, and read books. Although she was getting a lot of attention, I noticed she became a little clingier and always wanted to be close to us. I too felt the need to hold her close. Many nights, she begged me to sleep in my bed. On nights that she did sleep in my bed, I noticed she slept well. On nights she slept in her own bed, she would crawl into bed with me in the early mornings and snuggle tight. That benefitted us both. Spending time with her became more deliberate. I was also able to take advantage of the time I didn't have to work to take a few short trips away from home to break up the monotony. We developed a new routine or read and bought games and puzzles to do together. A few times, we were invited to see friends and relatives, but because we were socially distancing, this became a matter of stress for me, since I had to reject most of these invitations, which made my daughter angry, as it was an opportunity for her to be with other people. She wasn't always happy to hear that we were quarantining but understood that we didn't want to get sick or get anyone else sick.

This pandemic was scary for me as an adult, and it was important to me to make sure I protected my daughter from it as much as I possibly could. It has definitely changed the way I look at life. Making time for family is now my number one priority. I've always made excuses not to do things because I had to work. Now I close the shop for a day or a few hours, so I can attend her functions. I give her the opportunity to ask questions and voice her concerns as they come, and I explain to her as much as I can why we think differently. I tell her how much I love her and show her also how important she is to me. I'm encouraging her to be as independent as possible in preparation for a future without me hopefully in the distant future.

This pandemic has been a serious life-changing event, but it has made us stronger and more alert on how to appreciate the time we spend with each other.

Tonza Chapman
Mother of Kalista (six)*
Barber Shop Owner/Small Business Owner
*age at the onset of the pandemic

Making Memories

Life brings simple pleasures to us every day.
It is up to us to make them wonderful memories.

—*Cathy Allen*

March 2020. I was over halfway through the school year as a physical education (PE) and health teacher in a high school, and basketball season had just ended for me as a coach. This meant I was going to be able to spend more time at home. What I didn't realize was just how much time I would be spending there. I went from leaving my house at 6:30 a.m. and returning around 7:30 p.m. or later to being home 24/7. On those long pre-pandemic workdays, I missed my kids, but after a day of teaching, I got to be with my second family—my basketball family. Until the pandemic, though, I didn't realize how much I was missing at home.

As soon as basketball season ended, the pandemic hit, and we entered the uncharted waters of switching to remote learning. During that time, my wife and I were both trying to teach from home, lesson plan until the wee hours of the morning, and help our kindergartner and second grader navigate online learning while trying to wrangle our two-year-old who wanted to be on a device, too. To say that those moments were crazy is an understatement. There were tears both from the kids' frustration with the new version of school and missing friends and activities and from Kelly and me trying to wear our different hats (parent, teacher, academic support staff for our kids, therapist, wife, and chef). Seriously, do these kids ever stop eating?

But every so often, the reality of a global pandemic would penetrate the everyday madness. The world news was terrifying, and then it hit too close to home. I had a good friend lose her mother and almost lose her four-month-old son to COVID-19. I had a friend who lost a child through a tragic accident. As I sat at home isolated and exhausted from trying to be a teacher to five classes of high schoolers and my own two elementary-school-aged children—and keep Eliza from running naked through the living room on a Google Meet feed—I began to evaluate. Life can turn on a dime, without warning. Was I taking my time for granted? Was I really isolated in a pandemic, or was I just blind to the family that was sitting right next to me? What became laser-focus clear was that I had a choice. I could mourn what I was missing, be irritated and angry about the stress, and fear what might come, or I could start cherishing the crazy life I was living. I realized that too often I had taken for granted, and sometimes even resented the everyday mundane tasks of a working mom's life. I then asked myself: If something happened to me right now, how would my kids remember me? Was I doing enough to create memories with them? Were they memories that would leave them knowing how much I love them?

So, I chose to shift my focus. I came to enjoy helping my own kids with their schoolwork. It began to feel like a gift to be so involved in their daily school learning—something that teachers in normal times can never do with their own children. And without being able to pack our free time full of visits with friends, sports activities, playdates, shopping, and—did I mention more sporting events?—we were forced to slow down, think outside the box of expected entertainment, and find activities to do with the immediate family that we all enjoyed, or at least could tolerate without too much bickering.

We took daily walks around the neighborhood. We turned the local run-down tennis court into our own personal dog park. I learned that Charlie loves to cook—from pancakes, to cornbread, to grilled hotdogs, and to hamburgers. With much encouragement and lots of nervous tears, Kyla learned how to ride her bike. The proud look on her face was priceless. We learned that the gift of a trampoline was really a gift from God to break up the tedium of endless online learning. Our neighbor saw the kids riding their bikes so often that he built them a ramp. I then promptly learned that my littlest girl is fearless when she fell face first over the ramp and got right back on again. Being a working mom is important for me, both personally and financially. But this experience was turning out to be invaluable.

One family endeavor was to plan a sixteen-day family camping trip around upstate New York for the summer because, well, camping is outdoors, and safety is outside. It would be just us and our pop-up camper. The kids drew a map of New York state on a large poster board. They labelled the places we would visit and planned the best routes from one to the other. It was awesome to hear what each child envisioned for their "best trip ever" experience. Kyla wanted swimming pools; Charlie wanted to fish a lot, and Eliza wanted to find the coolest playgrounds. We took the time to explore what it was that excited them about traveling as a family. The trip was codesigned rather than Kelly and me schlepping our kids on a vacation filled with activities that we had planned for them, which made the planning process an amazing opportunity to create memories.

Working through the pandemic while also managing parenting, online school for our children, and childcare for a two-year-old was not easy. But as time went on, we found ever more creative ways to not only manage but create lasting, joyful memories. "Life brings simple pleasures to us every day"—a walk, dinner together, or laughing at the marshmallow stuck to your nose—and "it's up to us to make them wonderful memories." Although the pandemic was stressful and heartbreaking beyond words in many respects, it allowed me the gift of time with my family. I have created cherished memories, and I am a better person for it.

Amy Gilchrist
Mother of Charlie (eight), Kyla (six), and Eliza (two)*
Health and Physical Education Teacher
*ages at the onset of the pandemic

Discussion

B eing grateful is the art of being appreciative (Snyder and Lopez 460). It's finding light in the darkness and knowing that the presence of one may hide but not extinguish the presence of the other. Winter is an ideal example. Just as winter may seem bleak, it is also a renewal period; the earth, the plants, and many living creatures are at rest, preparing for spring. Similarly, as we are faced with moments of difficulty in our lives, we can find a spring of goodness, like a beautiful lavender crocus smiling through the snow, reminding us of the gifts in each situation. This paradox is present throughout our experiences. Even events such as family celebrations, which are generally considered positive, can contain some amount of stress. When we pause to consider how good times contain aspects of challenge, it's evident that hard times are no different, containing aspects of both enjoyment and difficulty. Our response to these experiences determines our reality as well as our emotions—a reality created from choice of perspective, where one can find either gifts or disappointments.

The four women in this section chose to focus on the aspects of their pandemic experience that they saw as beneficial and which brought joy to their lives in the process. Interestingly, their stories are not unique; they highlight the universality of gratitude across cultures. Stories from working mothers around the world—including in India (Mazumdar et al. 632), Colombia (Jablonska), and the US (Jablonska)—all highlight the ways mothers found gifts amid the pandemic challenges while maintaining their careers and showing us a way to enhance our lives even in difficult times.

What is their secret? How do these women thrive in the face of adversity? Choosing to be positive is their secret. Choice engages our opportunity to embrace our power. We may not get to choose everything about our circumstances, but we always get to choose how we react. We didn't choose a pandemic and the closing of schools, but we can decide how we will respond. The active power of choice is how each of these women found moments of enjoyment in their struggle. Consciously attending to and reflecting on our circumstances are the crux of gratitude. In actively seeking the good in every situation, gratitude emerges, bringing with it a sense of enjoying what is rather than lamenting what is not. It has been postulated that gratitude is a "cognitive process," requiring an acknowledgment of "a positive outcome" and then attributing that "positive outcome" to "an external source" (Emmons and McCullough 378). While practicing gratitude, the mind becomes attuned and develops an optimistic state that looks outside of ourselves. By looking outwards with positivity, the mind, which creates our reality, acknowledges the beauty that surrounds us. One way to experience gratitude is through a four-step procedure of noticing, thinking, feeling, and doing (Hussong). Explained more fully, the process requires us to realize the good in our life and reflect on it, become attuned to the sensations about the good we have, and finally recognize its value (Hussong).

The reality of a fork in the road, and the conscious choosing of a grateful path, was delineated by Amy, a teacher and mother of three young children: "I chose to shift my focus." In her decision, Amy pondered two worlds: one in which she could enjoy the process by "cherishing the crazy life I was living" or another in which she would come from a place of scarcity that lamented what she didn't have, leaving her "irritated and angry about the stress" and fearing "what might come." On the outside, it might appear that gratitude just happens to those with good circumstances. On closer examination, we can see it is a conscious choice. It is a choice to uplift the good aspects of any situation, altering the emotions we feel in response to what's happening around us. Another mother and corporate executive, Irina, discussed the benefits of choosing to appreciate her experience. In choosing what was important "to have fun and bond as a family," Irina "accepted the chaos," which allowed her to reach a "more relaxed and happier" state. This is not surprising, since gratitude has been linked with enhanced emotional and social wellbeing (Jans-Beken et al. 775).

The women in this chapter discovered that an advantage of their thankful focus was the gift of time with family, a theme found in other reports of mothers during the pandemic (Haskett et al. 855; Mazumdar et al. 632). For working mothers, the pandemic created the opportunity to engage with their children throughout the day, allowing them to savor moments they often missed due to work. As Stephanie, an accountant and mother of two revealed, she "felt grateful" to see her children for "breakfast, lunch, and dinner" as well as "between meetings or even during my calls." Other mothers spoke of being intentional with their time, appreciating the moments they had together in a new way. As Tonza, a small business owner and mother of one described, "spending time with [her daughter] became more deliberate." The pandemic allowed working mothers to cherish rich moments with their family.

Family time also provided profound meaning for mothers. The meaning they experienced was driven, in part, by the forced slowing down and existential realities highlighted during the pandemic. For Amy, the pondering of "how would my kids remember me?" along with the "forced slow down," resulted in "an amazing opportunity to create memories" with her family. These women were not alone in cherishing the slower lifestyle. Gratefulness for the forced slowdown was also found in a study of single mothers (Taylor et al. 354). The other aspect that helped to drive meaning was that millions of people were becoming ill and many were dying. "It became very clear to me that life, especially now, was too short, and we had to live each day to the fullest," said Tonza. Part of meaning in life is a feeling of having made an impact on the world, which will carry on even after we're gone (King and Hicks 567). The heightened existential perspective caused reflection and redirection for many women. Irina indicated, "I am more appreciative, present, relaxed and hyperaware of what really matters." This supports research from the pandemic showing that those who felt they had meaning in their life were less distressed than those who were lacking meaning (Schnell and Krampe 11). The pandemic pause, with its existential truths, reminded us that we can experience profound meaning, even in challenging times.

Steps to Re-imagining

Although it was a huge stressor, the pandemic provided the chance for working mothers to make new choices, develop an appreciative attitude, and create meaningful memories with their families. Irina shared how she is "still thankful" for the ways the pandemic altered her life and how it made her "more appreciative, present, relaxed, and hyperaware of what really matters." Her words remind us that changes in perspective, ushered in during a time of darkness, can continue to guide us to the light, even during less burdensome times. The fortitude of these four women in actively choosing gratitude as a path for improving their lives continues to create benefits for them, as they persist in finding the good in every situation and appreciate its contribution to their experience. Where does gratitude fit into your story?

Reflective Prompts

1. Where do you have a choice? Choices bring power and restore our advocacy. Consider places in your life where you might be able to take control to direct your path by choosing a new way of seeing things or doing things.

2. Understanding what holds meaning for you allows you to prioritize what's most important in your life. It makes choosing easier, thereby streamlining your time and energy into what you value the most. What holds the most meaning for you? How are you living in line with what holds the most meaning for you? Are you prioritizing what you value most?

3. Have you stopped to appreciate the little things today? It might be helpful to develop a daily gratitude practice, where you set a time each day to review what you are grateful for that day. For example, during dinner or as you tuck your children in each night, each of you could share a few things you appreciate from the day.

Works Cited

Eger, Edith. *The Choice: Embrace the Possible*. Scribner, 2017.

Emmons, Robert A., and Michael E. McCullough. "Counting Blessings Versus Burdens: An Experimental Investigation of Gratitude and Subjective Well-being in Daily Life." *Journal of Personality and Social Psychology*, vol. 84, no. 2, 2003, pp. 377-89.

Haskett, Mary E., et al. "'It Brought My Family More Together': Mixed-Methods Study of Low-Income U.S. Mothers During the

Pandemic." *Family Relations Interdisciplinary Journal of Applied Family Science*, vol. 71, no. 3, 2022, pp. 849-64.

Hussong, Andrea. "How to Practice Gratitude? Notice. Think. Feel. Do." *UNC*, 20 Nov. 2020, https://www.unc.edu/discover/how-to-practice-gratitude-notice-think-feel-do/. Accessed 31 May 2023.

Jablonska. Justine. "Parent, Employee, All of the Above? Eight Working Mothers Reflect on the Realities of Post-Pandemic Life." *McKinsey*, 6 May 2022, https://www.mckinsey.com/about-us/diversity/diversity-at-work/parent-employee-all-of-the-above-eight-working-mothers-on-the-realities-of-post-pandemic-life. Accessed 31 May 2023.

Jans-Beken, L., et al. "Gratitude and Health: An Updated Review." *The Journal of Positive Psychology*, vol. 15, no. 6, 2020, pp. 743-82.

King, Laura A., and Joshua A. Hicks. "The Science of Meaning in Life." *Annual Review of Psychology*, vol. 72, 2021, pp. 561-84.

Mazumdar, Ketoki, et al. "The Invisible Frontline Workers: Lived Experience of Urban Indian Mothers During the COVID-19 in India." *Journal of Gender Studies*, vol. 31, no. 5, 2022, pp. 623-38.

Park, Crystal L. "Making Sense of Meaning Literature: An Integrative Review of Meaning Making and its Effects on Adjustment to Stressful Life Events." *Psychological Bulletin*, vol. 136, no. 2, 2010, pp. 257-301.

Rubin, Gretchen. *The Happiness Project: Or Why I Spent a Year Trying to Sing in the Morning, Clean my Closets, Fight Right, Read Aristotle, and Generally Have More Fun.* Harper Collins Publishers, 2009.

Schnell, Tatjana, and Henning Krampe. "Meaning in Life and Self-Control Buffer Stress in Times of COVID-19: Moderating and Mediating Effects with Regard to Mental Distress." *Frontiers in Psychiatry*, vol. 11, 2020, pp. 1-16.

Snyder, C.R., and Shane J. Lopez. *Handbook of Positive Psychology*. Oxford University Press, 2002.

Taylor, Zoe E., et al. "Strengths of the Heart: Stressors, Gratitude, and Mental Health in Single Mothers During the COVID-19 Pandemic." *Journal of Family Psychology*, vol. 36, no. 3, 2022, pp. 346-57.

Tolle, Eckhart. *A New Earth: Awakening to Your Life's Purpose.* Penguin Books, 2016.

Chapter 6

Mothering in Community

Alone we can do so little; together we can do so much.

—*Helen Keller*

Social support has been defined as "the provision of assistance or comfort to others," which "may arise from any interpersonal relationship in an individuals' social network" (American Psychological Association). Lockdowns, online work, and social distancing all pushed us apart, removing many social supports. The five women in this section realized how much they cherished the bonds we share with others and sought to fill that void. We will hear from a speech language pathologist and new mother, laboring in the hospital as the pandemic lockdown took effect in the United States, who found a community of mothers through her work as a medical speech language pathologist. In contrast, an animator and new mom shares her experience of working from home while pregnant, highlighting the social isolation of new motherhood in a pandemic. Other mothers—a school nurse with an infant and a school principal with three children—actively sought to build a community within the confines of pandemic restrictions. Finally, a single mother of a young boy and owner of a birthing center describes the ways mothering moved into all aspects of our lives during the pandemic, an indication that just like birth, mothering is meant to be done in community. These women represent the vast range of what was experienced by working mothers during the COVID-19 pandemic. Managing one to three young lives, ranging in age from newborn to young adult, these moms traversed the social realm for themselves and their children. The insights of these women highlight the significance of our connection with one another and the value of mothering in community.

Behind Every Woman...

When women support each other, incredible things happen.

—Unknown

M arch 12, 2020, was the day my world changed—not just because it marked the day that the world declared COVID-19 to be a global pandemic but, because it was the day my first baby was born. Somewhere in the course of laboring for twenty-two hours, I was informed the hospital was going on lockdown due to COVID-19. My husband could stay because he was already there, but there would be no visitors. A *pandemic*. It was significant, no question. And, yet I had more important things to tend to. The details from hour to hour are blurry, but when the moment came, I remember the distinct sound of his first cry, his little body being placed on my chest, and the swift movements of doctors and nurses whisking him away to the Neonatal Intensive Care Unit (NICU) to join the other "preemies." The mix of emotions I felt would set the tone for the coming months: love, joy, fear, and resilience.

Our son was six weeks early and spent nine days in the NICU. Visitation became even more restrictive as the speed and extent of COVID-19's spread came to light. The nine days were long, but finally, hitting a key benchmark of four pounds, he was cleared to go home. The days after were also long, yet the months flew by. My husband and I hunkered down and worked together to keep our little one safe and thriving in an uncertain world. I was lucky to have his partnership and unwavering support then and in the months that have followed.

Although plenty of babies were born during this strange time, so too were mothers. First-time mothers, second-time mothers, single mothers—every iteration of motherhood is a rebirth. It is a gift, a challenge, and an opportunity. What would define us? Who would teach us and heal us when the world was upside down? Who would show up for me and for other working mothers grappling with the pandemic?

Fortunately for me, there are many people that come to mind—most notably my family and friends. Although I could write pages detailing the tremendous acts of kindness I experienced from them, I feel I owe a particular debt and gratitude to the powerful impact of working women and mothers who rallied around me at that time.

After five months of isolation, I returned to my job as a medical speech-language pathologist at a regional VA medical center. As the COVID-19 numbers at the hospital seesawed between manageable and abysmal, working moms like me wondered how we would handle it all. But the answer was right in front of us. In every hospital ward I peeked into, women were showing up for each other and their community. I realized this wasn't a fluke: Eighty per cent of healthcare workers and 83% of workers who provide social assistance (this includes childcare and emergency services) are women (US Bureau of Labor Statistics). Women were keeping things moving forward- like we always have, and always will. Women in leadership rallied around me, as did women col- leagues, who were compassionate and fiercely protective. They ensured that I was comfortable handling new personal protective equipment (PPE) procedures; they allocated appropriate breaks to pump between patients, and they gave me time to mentally adjust to the demands of performing high-risk procedures on potentially COVID-19-positive patients.

This support in turn allowed me to be better at my job. Yet even as I felt I was maximizing my potential in my professional career, for the first time in my life, this felt like a second priority. My identity, my conception of who I was as a person—a healthcare provider and a researcher—now had to morph to include my role as a mother. This shift of how I spent my time, the same twenty-four hours each day, and how I prioritized the dedication of those hours was informed by the community of working mothers who helped me navigate this new du- ality of purpose. I began to see working mothers through a new lens, having now stepped into their shoes. I asked questions of them. I shared resources. I stood in awe of all that they accomplished. I endeavored to make meaningful connections with other women and learn from their experiences.

It is a journey to become a working mother, and it can feel incredibly isolating. I remember a sinking feeling that I was failing in those early days, even while having incredible support. But the women in my family, workplace, and community helped raise me up and support me in my new role. I began to realize that mothers need nurturing in the same way children do. So many of the skills I acquired were through the wise tongues of other women who had trodden a similar path before me—whether it was a fool-proof toddler recipe from my mom (also a speech-language pathologist), a sleep training strategy from a colleague, or a nudge to incorporate a self-care routine from a friend so I could feel a little more like myself.

The pandemic revealed to me the many miles we still must travel as women in the workforce, but it also illustrated what we can achieve together, even when the world is in a state of chaos. I found this to be incredibly inspiring—something I drew strength from on days when I felt exhausted. I learned that standing in solidarity with other working women was incredibly powerful. And with that power came opportunity—to advocate, to support, to protect one another, and to find ways to preserve ourselves from burning out. When women support one another, incredible things happen.

Sonia Mehta, M.S. CCC-SLP
Mother of Julian Desai Backus
Medical Speech-Language Pathologist

New Office

found out I was pregnant around Christmas of 2019. At the time, I was a couple of months into a new job at Nickelodeon animation studios after eight years of show-running the Disney animated show *Star vs. the Forces of Evil*. I was getting to know the ways of a new studio, making friends, and decorating my office. At Disney, my office had a big window, but at Nickelodeon, my new office did not. So, I decided to make it so fun I wouldn't mind. Floor to ceiling, my office was covered by fan art kids had sent me, art books, and throw pillows. It was cute!

By March of 2020, I was starting to show, and I knew I needed to tell my coworkers. I was so nervous. In retrospect, I don't know why. Most of my bosses at Nickelodeon are women with kids of their own, but it was a new job, and I didn't want to disappoint anyone. I showed up with cupcakes, gathered everyone, and told them the news. Of course, they were great about it, and I felt very happy. That was a Friday. The following Monday, I was called into a big studio meeting. Everyone was going to work from home for two weeks because of COVID-19.

It's now January 2022, and my son is almost a year and a half. I haven't been back to the office. No one has, really. All the animation studios have been closed, with everyone working from home. I think about how weird it'll be if I ever get to go back. I imagine the post-it notes sitting around from March 2020. The to-do lists. Snack wrappers in the garbage bin. The whole thing feels like some Ray Bradbury story. The computers live on while the humans are quarantined. I'm just glad I had the wherewithal to take food home. My early pregnant self was keeping a lot of snacks around. I have a friend who left a bag of oranges on his desk. I can't imagine what they look like now.

My life feels very changed; how much of that change is because of the new baby vs. the pandemic is hard to know. As a person who works in animation, you might imagine a bunch of socially awkward nerds sitting around drawing in dark cubicles. But I would describe us more as artsy fun nerds who love to make imaginative stuff for kids. Every animated show takes a crew of around fifty to make. It's a very collaborative process, and a lot of the people I work with I've known since college. It's a tight-knit community. I miss everyone so much. I also feel like I missed a lot of experiences I was excited to have. I was excited to go to work pregnant. None of my friends saw me pregnant, not even my mom. That still bums me out. I was excited to show my new baby off. I pictured taking my little dude around in a stroller through the office at lunch when I was on maternity leave.

Yet I have seen the benefits of being a new parent when your whole work is work from home. I just about never had to pump. I found I could breastfeed and draw at the same time. I breastfed for a whole year. I don't think I could have kept it up that long if I was in an office. Without all the social interactions, I find the workday is shorter. But I also don't feel like myself without those social interactions. I used to have a hectic life and prided myself in being a "weekend warrior": a fifty-six-hour work-week into a jam-packed weekend of friends and fun (e.g., art shows, concerts, parties, hiking up mountains, beach days, and brunch). I knew having a baby would mean slowing down in some ways, but I also pictured being the mom who would wear my baby in a sling and do it all anyway.

Now, my weekends have no plans. I love the time I spend with my little dude, but it's also hard not to feel like we are missing out on something. But just what it is, I can't tell you.

Daron Nefcy
Mom
Creator of the show Star vs. the Forces of Evil. Animation
Showrunner, Writer, Artist, Producer, etc.

It Takes a Village

It takes a village to raise a child

—Unknown

Our daughter Addison was born in December 2019. When the pandemic hit, I was still on maternity leave from my job as a Family nurse practitioner at a college health clinic. At this time, in the early stages of the pandemic, family provided the most support. My stepdaughter Lindsey was in high school, which went remote. Having her at home meant that she could watch Addison when I went back to work remotely in April 2020. This set up would never have been possible if it hadn't been for our unique family structure. It was a blessing to have Lindsey in our lives to help with Addison and as another person to talk to during the lockdown period. We would go running together and cook new recipes; I feel like our family bond was strengthened during this period.

In the fall of 2020, I changed jobs, taking on my current role as a high school nurse. This meant I had to go into work each day outside of my home, which created new challenges related to childcare. A large part of my job entailed contact tracing, notifying individuals when they were exposed to COVID-19 and keeping spreadsheets of quarantine times in addition to my usual nurse-related duties. My job as a school nurse exploded with the new COVID-19-related protocols, all while I was struggling to balance Addison's needs as she started daycare. I decided a home daycare was the right fit, and this worked well until she developed biting behaviors. During this time, I was grateful to have a past preschool teacher in my group of mom friends who helped me to handle this new parenting challenge. Ultimately, we had to change daycare providers in the middle of the pandemic, which was a difficult transition, but we were lucky to have the support of early intervention providers.

In the new daycare, Addison experienced many illnesses—from fifth disease, to COVID-19, to varicella. The constant COVID-19 quarantines at daycare due to class exposures meant that Addison only attended daycare about 50 percent of the time. This meant I had to take a lot of sick days and lean on our extended family for help. Then COVID-19 came to our house (January 2022). Working in a high school, I figured our family would eventually get COVID-19, since I was exposed to many cases each day. Fortunately, we all made it through the illness with mild symptoms and most importantly our village was there to support us—bringing us food and supplies and providing deeply needed moral support during those ten days of isolation.

A huge source of encouragement over the last two years has been a close group of fellow mom friends that I met in a breastfeeding support group shortly after Addison was born. We were lucky to first meet in person before the pandemic hit, and we stayed connected as the group continued online during lockdown. As the weather improved with spring, we met up outside for walks. Parks and playgrounds were closed, so we had to be creative in finding places to meet outdoors. In the summer of 2021, despite COVID-19 still being present, we had a much-needed moms' weekend away. I can't even begin to describe how much this group of women has helped me to maintain my sense of self while being a new mom during the pandemic. I also feel blessed to have had a close friend from graduate school in my "pod" for most of the pandemic. She has a son who is nine months older than Addison, and her empathetic advice on raising a newborn to a toddler and weekend trips with the little rascals truly allowed me to maintain my sanity. I'm so grateful to have a committed group of generous and thoughtful women in my life.

To this day our village continues to provide for us. We are fortunate that our family watches Addison frequently so we can get errands done, go on dates, and maintain our interests. The pandemic has reinforced that I still need time for each part of me: the mom raising her kids, the mom who is a school nurse, the mom who is an athlete, and the mom who is a wife and friend, to name a few. I consider myself incredibly lucky to have had a better pandemic experience than many working moms, and I have our village to thank. We made a choice to have a close-knit pod, even during the pandemic, and for me, that choice was our lifeline.

Erika Almquist, MSN, RN, FNP
Mother of Addison (three months)*
Stepmother of Lindsey (fifteen) and Kayleigh (twenty-three)*
School Nurse
*ages at the onset of the pandemic

The "Unprecedented" Present

In a world of noise, confusion, and conflict, it is necessary
that there be places of silence, inner discipline, and peace.
In such places love can blossom.

—Thomas Merton

My school district called for an early dismissal, and I said good-bye to my students on a Wednesday at 12:00 p.m. in March of 2020. Like every day, I wished them a good afternoon, reminded them to do their homework, and closed with, "I'll see you to-morrow." Never did I imagine that it would be almost a year until I would see their faces (in person) again. Such a harsh, unplanned, unprepared dismissal led to emotions of confusion, fear, disbelief for students as well as for my family and myself. I returned home to my children and glued myself to the news and social media. I was initially disconnected with my family, as I searched for an answer as how to protect them in "this un-precedented time" that we needed to "navigate"—two sayings that I have grown to despise due to their overuse resulting in empty jargon.

In the following days, my husband, also victim to the media, covered head to toe in protective gear, headed to the grocery store to scavenge what was left on the shelves: cans of Chef Boyardee, processed foods and toilet paper... lots and lots of toilet paper. His objective was to provide, keep us safe, and take care of his own.

The days passed, the news shared deaths all across the world, and my little family of five stayed together, locked in our home with nothing to do. The kids busied themselves with social media and video games. I worked and tried to stay connected with my students via messages and emails. However, that all became monotonous. We are typically a busy family—sports, work, social life, and large family gatherings. We are constantly on the move. I follow school schedules and sports schedules. My entire life was filled with happy chaos and noise and conflict. And now we had quiet.

My son having started his first year in college was home, back in the shared bedroom with his younger brother—not exactly what he had in mind as his first year at University of Rhode Island. My little guy, always outdoors where he feels most happy, was locked in and growing angrier as time passed. My daughter, an eighth grader and social, was stuck in her bedroom surrounded by pictures of her social life. And me, I felt trapped by this widespread disease. My family was becoming infected. I watched the kids and myself get sicker and sicker by the lack of life because of COVID-19. I cried for friends who lost so much, but I was watching my kids get lost.

School resumed for my children, virtually. The three of them in three stages of their academic career engaged in the same rote cookie-cutter lessons while in their jammies, not having showered or brushed. They were passively going to school and just as I raised them to do, completed the assignment in spite of their lack of interest, engagement, or enthusiasm.

I needed to make a decision. Take the chance of getting COVID-19 or allow COVID-19 to continue to suck the life out of myself and my family. I got up, got dressed, and went to work. I called my family, a small group, and we gathered on sunny days in my backyard to eat and talk and drink. We didn't have a reason, just a realization that we all needed people. We played monopoly with the kids and had fruitful conversations about life. We told stories, looked through old pictures, and worked on projects together. We hiked, went on walks, and watched movies. We were a captive audience. We connected, got to know one another, and philosophized. Life was quiet and simple, so I began to appreciate what COVID-19 was giving to me and my family.

Months passed as I indulged in the wonderfulness afforded by the pandemic. I loved the love that was filling my home and growing greater every day. And what I loved even more was that I could enjoy it, quietly, without all of the noise my life had grown accustomed to.

However, slowly the world began to reopen and the group that filled my days in the backyard began to dwindle. "My people" started to go back to living. I had extremely mixed feelings about this. I certainly was glad to go back to normal, but the abnormal had started to grow on me. During that time of quiet, I could be present and committed. It didn't take long for the noise to begin again, and our lives were governed once again by busy schedules.

Looking back, I realize after that I did do right by my children. Although they lost in terms of schooling—virtual education is not replacement for a true, well-rounded education—my children and I gained so much. When I returned to my urban high school, I was greeted by children with increased mental health needs who were unable to socialize and had lost so much learning and development because of the pandemic. I realized that my decision to bring socialization into my home during the most isolated time was the best decision I could have made for my family and for myself. There was so much lost as a result of the pandemic; however, I am grateful for it. For a short time, life quieted, and in that silence, I was gifted with peace and love. Typically, a work junkie, I am changed as a result of the pandemic. Now that life has resumed, I force myself to find the quiet so the love can continue to blossom.

Beth Furnari
*Mother of AJ (eighteen), Mike (fifteen), and Olivia (thirteen)**
High School Principal
*age at the onset of the pandemic

Mothering as Ecological Restoration

You were wild once here. Don't let them tame you.

—Isadora Duncan

E cological restoration: "the process of assisting the recovery of an ecosystem that has been degraded, damaged or destroyed" (Society for Ecological Restoration, 2023).

Life as sole caretaker, provider, disciplinarian, and nurturer has been my normal for nine years. During these years, I not only created and mothered a human but also a business—a business that, much like the child, has grown to proportions that surprise and delight me and that revolves around pregnancy and birth. A business I started because I needed a Village. This business involves a continuous shifting of daily structure to accommodate the spontaneity of birth—the shuffling of my own baby/toddler/kiddo to a neighbor's couch or out to suburban family members. We are a dynamic game of Tetris, a relentless arranging and rearranging of the rapidly falling shapes of my days and nights.

I have developed a system over the years to deftly organize the unpredictable. Navigating a global pandemic with larger, structural pieces falling felt somewhat manageable to me. I was familiar with uncertainty, not terribly flustered by sudden major shifts of schedules, and employed a familiar fluidity when structure fell by the wayside. What I was not prepared for was the time together—the 24/7 with no breaks, no one to run interference, and, no place to bring him, nowhere to be all day every day. Riding this wave with him through the second, third, and fourth grade has been tumultuous but not without gifts.

There were moments I resented him and moments I hated me. There were full days he spent on the iPad while I cried in another room, days we cried together. We wrestled to work out our own agitation—hugging too tightly and yelling at one another in ways we had never done before. Our own unique anxieties took form. We got a puppy and spent endless hours snuggling. We turned the screens off halfway through the day and found outdoor spaces to explore. We smashed ice and climbed rocks and took epic bike rides when the weather broke. We worked through big emotions and found joy amid the confusion and peace amid the chaos. We synched up with one another in the way that only this level of intensity demanded of us.

I began to find ways to love the unstructured time that we hadn't experienced since his infancy. Most of the initial pressures started to melt away until the weight was exclusively financial. I began to sense an innate, deeply suppressed (or perhaps simply untapped) connection to the rhythms of our days and nights: eating when we were truly hungry rather than on the go, sleeping and waking at times our bodies decided were appropriate rather than the alarm heralding the beginnings and endings of our days, and having all of the time and space for the natural rhythms of our systems and honoring them fully. It was a call back to nature, which we were able to answer.

The pandemic has forced mothering into all spaces. My work did not hit a hard stop when the rest of the world did. Birth never stops. My child has always come with me to work, always had a space of his own carved out within mine. It is the necessity of single parenthood; my kid is with me everywhere. To witness this inclusion of children in all spaces out of necessity, as parents pivoted to work and school from home, was liberating for me. I felt a twinge of solidarity. We blurred the lines between mothering time and working time, allowing our rhythms to dictate how we made this happen while meeting both of our demands. The overwhelming demands of these two as separate—mothering and working—somehow settled into something that felt more natural as the two collided. We are taking back our village, first with our children and next with the small groups we formed as the pandemic went on and on.

The presence of children in all spaces became normalized as our mothering seeped outwards. We have been here the whole time. We simply compartmentalized our mothering and made it "other" to the rest of our responsibilities as though it could be extracted and isolated from anything else we ever do. Mother is a verb. It is a continuous commitment to nurturing. In nurturing one another, we nurture the planet and, by extension, humanity as a whole. I feel community so profoundly as we continue to work toward new ways of surviving and thriving, caretaking and refilling one another's cups. How I wish I were witnessing it translate across our social structures and systems.

My work has cultivated within me a profound understanding that ceremonial birth is ecological restoration. That in honoring one another as members of a lineage that begins in the same home, the womb, we can remember and fully connect with the pulsation of the life force. We can embrace the shifting of the old paradigm and actively participate in the rebuilding of a new one.

The mothers of the world have the power to restore homeostasis—to return the balance where things have come loose, to gather pieces that have fallen through cracks, to transform what has been destroyed, and to transmute suffering, fear, and pain into connection, community, and compassion.

There have been two years and counting of uncertainty, and I do not have a second thought about sleeping in a little longer on mornings my child expresses needing it. I have no issue with taking him in to school a little later or pulling him out altogether because there is fresh snow, or the day is begging for us to embrace it. We have so much more to learn together. We have the opportunity to restore our life rhythms, not just within ourselves and our children but within our communities at large.

This level of connection and presence is a gift. It is something I always felt burning deeper under the skin—a shift toward the recovery of a wisdom as well as an integrity that has been all but destroyed by the constructs of a culture that values how hard we work over how hard we play, how plugged in we are to technologies over how plugged in we are to nature and one another, and how much we consume over how much we cultivate.

Birthing and mothering are ecological restoration. We are not meant to be doing either in isolation. I take this wisdom and root deeper. With my child at my side or on my back, my mothering spills over relentlessly, generously, and wildly like fast growing vines seeking sources of nourishment. Entangling in community. Rooting in rhythm. I cannot shake the feeling I am deep in the taking back of something I didn't fully realize I had given away.

Rebecca J. Mercurio, CD DONA, LMT, RYT
Mother of Gideon (seven)*
Certified Birth Doula
Owner/Operator at Whole Nine Wellness
Owner/Creative Director at Cary House Buffalo
*age at the onset of the pandemic

Discussion

Humans are social creatures. We have survived for tens of thousands of years as a result of our cooperation and interdependence (Apicella and Silk R447; Hare and Woods). During the pandemic, COVID-19 stripped us of our human strength by forcing us apart, as we made changes to protect one another. The virus preyed on our innate wiring: the inner drive to connect with others. Mothers were forced to navigate the unknown terrain of how social interaction could affect grandparents and vulnerable children (Walker 213). As we were forced apart, the paradox of the term "social distancing" was felt. How can one be social and distant at the same time? The forced separation from others created a tsunami of mental distress in mothers (Kotlar 32; Babore). Just as premature babies who are not held have worse relationship scores and sleep compared to those who are held (Feldman et al. 61) and older adults who are lonely and isolated experience more health problems (National Institute of Aging), the women in this chapter realized they needed to find ways to bond; their health depended on it.

All five women in this chapter discuss the significance of social connection in their lives. These women determined that their health depended not only on implementing measures to prevent getting COVID-19 or spreading it to others, but also on creating social support within these confines. One mother who acutely saw the withering of her family amid the lockdown was Beth, a school principal and mother of three. Observing that her "family was becoming infected," Beth became aware that either COVID-19 would make them ill, or the COVID-19-imposed social isolation would "suck the life out" of herself and her family. Younger working mothers were more affected by the social isolation than seasoned working mothers (Hadjicharalambous et al. 49). Daron, an animator and a new mother, discusses the pros and cons of working from home. Although the "workday is shorter without those social interactions," she notices that she doesn't feel like herself. Research highlights the benefits of social connection for parents and children, with stronger parental social support being linked to improved parent and child wellbeing (McConnell et al. 688).

Seasoned mothers had an easier time identifying what was wrong. Beth, for example, realized that she "needed people." Mothering does not occur in a vacuum; we need each other for support, learning, and sharing. Even mothers who were able to give birth in the year before the pandemic benefitted from the ability to form connections with other new moms before the shutdown. One such mother was Erika, a school nurse and mom to a daughter born in December 2019, who describes her "village," which included a "group of women" she met before the pandemic lockdown in March 2020. These women adapted their interactions to fit within the health guidelines, which helped Erika to maintain a "sense of self" during the challenging days of early motherhood and the pandemic. Both of these mothers saw that they needed others and created "pandemic pods." Pandemic pods were groups of individuals that formed in the socially restricted days of the pandemic to provide connection and support for one another (Chiu). Individuals in the pod decided upon the rules all members would follow, such as mask wearing when out in public, in order to decrease their risk of spreading COVID-19 to one another (Chiu). Erika discusses how her pod was her "lifeline," whereas Beth states that bringing "socialization into my home during the most isolated times was the best decision I could have made."

The social isolation was especially challenging for mothers who were born during the pandemic. The psychological adaptation to the mother role, also known as matrescence, was obstructed due to limited social contact (Gibson; Sacks). Many pregnant, employed mothers were unable to share the experience of carrying a child in their womb with their co-workers. Sitting at a computer hides a pregnant belly, whereas in person, the beautiful round bump is on display for all to see. Daron laments these missed experiences she was "excited to have" that never happened, including friends and family seeing her pregnant as well as taking her "little dude around in a stroller through the office at lunch." Pregnant moms were grieving, dealing with the loss of experiences that are milestones in life. The experience of new mother grief related to these missed experiences has been found in studies of pregnant and new moms during the COVID-19 pandemic (Kinser et al. 659; LoGiudice and Bartos 10-11). These milestone moments of sharing pregnancy and new motherhood with one's community are needed to usher in the transformation from individual to mother—the ultimate social connection uniting a woman with a new life that is dependent on her for survival.

New mothers also lacked the ease of forming a social network of other new moms. They never got to build their community of mothers in person through baby classes, new mom groups, and feeding-support programs. If services like breastfeeding support were offered, they were often provided online during the pandemic (Koerting; Schindler-Ruwisch and Phillips 264). In the virtual world, there's no way to have a smooth group discussion. The nonverbal cues and social imitation present during our in-person interactions are missing, resulting in silence or moments of speaking at the same time. These pandemic alterations along with working from home left Daron feeling as if she were "missing out on something," but she wasn't sure what it was. She had never been able to experience mothering in community.

For new mothers who were still working outside the home, it was a different experience. Sonia, a medical speech-language pathologist and new mother of a preterm infant, was able to experience "nurturing" from other "working women and mothers who rallied around" her as she returned to work in the hospital. This nurturing between mothers is also noted by Rebecca, a birth center owner and mother of an elementary-school-aged boy. She states, "Mother is a verb. It is continuous commitment to nurturing." Rebecca also reminds us that mothering, just like birth, is not "meant to be" done "in isolation." Pandemic restrictions created a chasm that new mothers had to navigate to find the community they needed. In-person work helped to reduce the isolation and bring working mothers together in support of one another.

Another group of mothers that felt the isolation of social distancing was single moms, who struggled to be everything to their children without the regular supports of family and friends. "Life as a sole caretaker, provider, disciplinarian, and nurturer" was a game of "Tetris" for Rebecca. In normal times, she had a network of "suburban family members" that helped out. This network disappeared with the pandemic, leaving Rebecca on duty "24/7" with "no breaks." These lost connections along with having to take on additional roles (such as teacher) during the pandemic have been echoed in other mothers' accounts of the pandemic (Weaver and Swank 139). Stripped of their social support networks, mothers became acutely aware of how their relationships with others helped to maintain their health—whether it be mental health through others lending a listening ear or physical health through watching another's children, allowing a weary mom to sleep or take a quiet walk. The pandemic reminded us that mothering is a community endeavor.

Steps to Re-imagining

Each of the five mothers in this chapter highlight the significance of social support as an essential lifeline by which to navigate our everyday lives. Social connections provide a rescue boat when we're caught in a storm, a sun to help us grow, and a hot air balloon to lift us when we need a new perspective. Through shared moments with others, we create collective memories that bind us together. We need others to help us mark important transition moments in life, such as becoming a mother or a child going off to college. The insights of these mothers remind us that we need to reach out to others, strengthen the connections we have, and continue to grow new relationships. When we mother in community, we find great joy in our parenting journey.

Reflection Questions

1. Consider the relationships you have in your life right now. Who do you feel closest to? What makes you feel close to them? What can you do to strengthen the bond you have with those around you?

2. If you want to have friends, you have to be the kind of friend others want to have. What can you do to be a better friend to those you care about? Do you have a special skill or talent you could share with them? Can you lend a listening ear?

3. Experiences with others bind us together. Who in your social circle might you share a new experience with this week? Maybe

you want to try a new restaurant together. Perhaps you could go take a walk at a park you've never been to.

4. Friends listen to each other. Have you taken the time to genuinely listen to what is going on in a friend's life? Practice listening without problem solving. You are not there to solve the problem; rather, you are there to support them through what they are experiencing. Try active listening where you reflect back what they say, help them place this situation in the context of their life as you know it, and give them words to describe what they are feeling.

5. Building new connections is just as important as maintaining the ones we have already. Do you have a hobby that you enjoy? Is there a local group that brings others with that same interest together? Joining groups that have similar interests is a great way to meet others and form new social connections.

Works Cited

American Psychological Association. "Social Support." *APA Dictionary of Psychology*, https://dictionary.apa.org/social-support. Accessed 4 June 2023.

Apicella, Coren L., and Joan B. Silk. "The Evolution of Human Cooperation." *Current Biology*, vol. 29, no. 11, 3 June 2019, pp. R425-R473.

Babore, Alessandra, et al. "Mothers' and Children's Mental Health During the COVID-19 Pandemic Lockdown: The Mediating Role of Parenting Stress." *Child Psychiatry & Human Development*. https://doi.org/10.1007/s10578-021-01230-6.

Chiu, Allyson. "A Pandemic Pod Could Help You Get through Winter, Experts Say. Here's How to Form One." *The Washington House*, 14 Oct. 2020, https://www.washingtonpost.com/lifestyle/wellness/pandemic-pod-winter-covid/2020/10/14/214ed65c-0d63-11eb-b1e8-16b59b92b36d_story.html. Accessed 4 June 2023.

Duncan, Isadora. *Isadora Speaks: Uncollected Writings and Speeches of Isadora Duncan*. City Light Books, 1981.

Feldman, Ruth, et al. "Maternal-Preterm Skin-to-Skin Contact Enhances Child Physiologic Organization and Cognitive Control Across the First 10 Years of Life." *Biological Psychiatry*, vol. 75, no. 1, 2014, pp. 556-64.

Gibson, Caitlin. "The Strange and Lonely Transformation of First-Time Mothers in the Pandemic." *The Washington Post*, 3 June 2021, https://www.washingtonpost.com/lifestyle/on-parenting/first-time-mothers-pandemic-transformation/2021/06/01/026e1c7a-b71d-11eb-96b9-e949d5397de9_story.html. Accessed 4 June 2023.

Hadjicharalambous, Demetris, et al. "The Impact of the Covid-19 Social Isolation Measures on the Resilience and Quality of Life of Working Mothers." *Social Education Research*, vol. 2, no. 1, 2021, pp. 41-51.

Hare, Brian H., and Vanessa Woods. "Humans Owe Our Evolutionary Success to Friendship. Cooperation is the Key to Long Term Survival." *Popular Science*, 21 July 2020, https://www.popsci.com/story/science/survival-of-the-friendliest/. Accessed 4 June 2023.

Kinser, Patricia A., et al. "Depression, Anxiety, Resilience, and Coping: The Experience of Pregnant and New Mothers During the First Few Months of the COVID-19 Pandemic." *The Journal of Women's Health*, vol. 30, no. 5, 2021, pp. 654-64.

Koerting, Katrina. "COVID-19 Pandemic Pushes CT Breastfeeding Services Online." *Stamford Advocate*, 3 Sept. 2021, https://www.stamfordadvocate.com/local/article/COVID-19-pandemic-pushes-CT-breastfeeding-16420229.php. Accessed 4 June 2023.

Kotlar, Bethany, et al. "The Impact of the COVID-19 Pandemic on Maternal and Perinatal Health: A Scoping Review." *Reproductive Health*, vol. 18, no. 10, pp. 1-39.

LoGiudice, J.A. & Bartos, S. (2022). Mixed-Methods Study of the Experience of Pregnancy During the COVID-19 Pandemic. *Journal of Obstetric, Gynecologic & Neonatal Nursing – JOGNN*. 51(5), 548-557. https://doi.org/10.1016/j.jogn.2022.07.001

McConnell, David, et al. "From Financial Hardship to Child Difficulties: Main and Moderating Effects of Perceived Social Support." *Child: Care, Health and Development*, vol. 37, no. 5, 2021, pp. 679-91.

National Institute on Aging. "Loneliness and Social Isolation - Tips for Staying Connected." *NIA*, https://www.nia.nih.gov/health/loneliness-and-social-isolation-tips-staying-connected#:~:text=Social%20isolation%20is%20the%20lack,while%20being%20with%20 other%20people. Accessed 4 June 2023.

Sacks, Alexandra. "The Birth of a Mother." *The New York Times*, 8 May 2017,https://www.nytimes.com/2017/05/08/well/family/the-birth-of-a-mother.html?_r=1. Accessed 4 June 2023.

Schindler-Ruwisch, J. and Kathryn E. Phillips. "Breastfeeding During a Pandemic: The Influence of COVID-19 on Lactation Services in the Northeastern United States." *Journal of Human Lactation*, vol. 37, no. 2, 2021, pp. 260-68.

Society for Ecological Restoration. "What Is Ecological Restoration?" 2023. https://www.ser-rrc.org/what-is-ecological-restoration/#:~:-text=Ecological%20restoration%20is%20the%20process,environ-ment%20as%20a%20functional%20unit. Accessed 9 June 2023.

US Bureau of Labor Statistics. "Labor Force Statistics from the Current Population Survey." *US Bureau*, 20 Jan. 2022, https://www.bls.gov/cps/cpsaat18.htm. Accessed 4 June 2023.

Walker, Kimberly K. "Mothers' Sources and Strategies for Managing COVID-19 Uncertainties during the Early Pandemic Months." *Journal of Family Communication*, vol. 21, no. 3, 2021, pp. 205-22.

Weaver, Jo Lauren, and Jacqueline M. Swank. "Parents' Lived Experiences with the COVID-19 Pandemic." *The Family Journal: Counseling and Therapy for Couples and Families*, vol. 29, no. 2, 2021, pp. 136-42.

Chapter 7

Growing Stronger

*Maybe you have to know the darkness before you
can appreciate the light.*
—*Madeleine L'Engle*

Surviving something and deeply reflecting on that experience can be
a catalyst for mentally and physically thriving (Tedeschi and
Calhoun 1). This chapter demonstrates how its seven contributors
were not immune to the emotional lulls and hurdles of the pandemic, but
how through facing these obstacles, they used personal strength as a
mechanism to grow as mothers and in their careers. Each woman can-
didly shares the difficulties of her day-to-day life during the pandemic
and discusses their feelings of anxiety, worry, panic, and fear. It certainly
wasn't without struggle that the pandemic led these women to their
insights.

This chapter may best be thought of as the backstage door to a stronger you. Growth can be messy, yet it is a propelling force forward, even
through the toughest times. The voices of these seven women reveal the
grit involved in paving the winding path of their journey. Their careers
span the following professions: state detective, academic professor, executive producer, clinical psychologist, primary care nurse practitioner,
hairstylist and salon owner, and district level school administrator and
technology educator. At the outset of the pandemic, their children
ranged in age from one-month-old twins to teenage twins, with many
having school-aged children.

Alone in a House
Full of People

Breathe, this is just a chapter, not your whole story.

—*SC Lourie*

I have twins. They are my only children. My teens were sixteen when the pandemic started, turned seventeen as they rounded out a ten-day quarantine after testing positive for COVID-19 (before they could be vaccinated), and celebrated eighteen after being vaccinated and boosted and finishing five days of quarantine due to round two of COVID-19. When the pandemic first started, my kids lost their bonds at school, at work, and at their extracurricular activities. Teens thrive on social interaction. In essence, they lost their connection to themselves. They were left with mom and dad, typically not most teen-first choice for whom they would like to spend time with. During the months that followed, there were many tense moments in my house, many arguments, lots of tears, and a great amount of worry. As I tried to balance my work and family life, I often felt like my home was falling apart at the seams, and I was all alone. As a Latino family, we thrive and rely on family support. Gathering with extended family is the norm, and this was instantaneously stripped away during COVID-19. For me, the extra support that I would have normally relied on to help me through these difficult transitions was not available. The unconditional love that younger kids impart after their tantrums and meltdowns is absolutely not part of how teens deal with their anxieties and stressors.

My preliminary worries centered around the influence of too much screen time and social media and trying to help them engage during online learning. I was concerned that this behavior during such critical years before college could impact study habits, social interactions, and opportunities, like summer college camps. Initially, I was hopeful that the lockdown would be short lived, and things would return back to normal within a brief amount of time. I indulged in watching more Netflix than usual as a way to bond with my teens. I sat through things like *Tiger King* while wondering how many brain cells I lost trying to enjoy some joint laughs; binge-watched *Criminal Minds* when I could during the day so we could have something to talk about over dinners; and struggled through *Love Is Blind* so that we could engage in conversations about relationships. Despite these efforts, I noticed fairly quickly that there were some negative coping mechanisms happening in our house. We were all gaining weight. There also seemed to be much more sadness and a lot more tense and argumentative interactions between us all. It became my fault when SAT prep courses had to be via Zoom, when they couldn't secure a sooner appointment for their driver's test, when the Wi-Fi couldn't support all our online needs, or when we couldn't get an appointment for the acne that was now out of control. They had many reasons to be upset—milestones that could not happen as they should have—and mom was the easiest one to blame. I saw my teens struggling, and I didn't know how to fix it. They wanted to be back in school with friends. They wanted to play sports and feel the excitement of the cheers. They wanted to not take their first advanced placement exams sitting in our dining room. And I couldn't write a letter to make those things happen.

Although I didn't have the worry of young children that would need me to sit with them as they logged into an online classroom, I did have to motivate my kids to be present while learning. I would see them watching TikTok while they were "in class." I had to discourage their logging into class from their bed. I tried to model what I wanted them to do as we all worked and learned from home, even as I struggled to keep myself from drowning. In all honesty, there were plenty of days that I wanted to log into a meeting from my bedroom. And although I never did that, I often closed my bedroom door and cried silently. In our household, it was an ongoing battle for personal space and being cognizant of who was online during what times so that we wouldn't interrupt class, work, or a meeting. These open-house concepts were not created with multiple people working and schooling from home in mind. Living, learning, and working together 24/7 stripped away privacy in ways that we had never dealt with before, and privacy is extremely important to teens. This lack of control contributed to yet another challenge for us to navigate. Thankfully, prior to the pandemic, we all had mental health therapists in place, but finding a private space to have a session where no one could hear what you were talking about became tricky. They often would go out and sit in the car to have their sessions. I needed to make sure that any errands I needed the car for would not interrupt this private time—a compromise I was willing to make. At the height of the pandemic, I often found myself sitting alone in my living room, feeling like I was such a failure as a mom. My kids have always been loving and kind, but as teenagers navigate hormones, unfamiliar situations, and a lack of control, they can be intentionally hurtful and sometimes downright mean. The pandemic gave them many reasons to be just that, and I became the primary recipient.

Teens want to be grown and pretend not to need adults, but my kids needed me even more than I realized during that time. They were afraid, but too scared to be open about their anxieties. During the pandemic, our teens were mourning the loss of many significant moments—like ring dances, proms, school concerts, games, and plays. All these events they weren't going to get to do over. These are critical years where self-growth happens and decision-making skills are learned. They discover how to balance the wants and needs of friends and families and navigate the responsibilities that come with getting their first job. This was all put on hold or just stripped away. My teens were sad and angry about all of that. And I felt helpless because as a parent, I couldn't make up for all that they were missing out on. I battled with an endless barrage of work so that I could try to also be present and available for kids who most of the time wanted nothing to do with their mom. As busy as I was with work, the pandemic was also one of my most unproductive times. I was so preoccupied and concerned about my kids. As a mom of teens, I was trying to figure out how much they could mentally handle while also toeing that line myself. Those were lonely times. We were all afraid and vulnerable, but I often pretended to have strength for them. I was aware of negative coping mechanisms (like cutting and substance misuse) and tried to encourage self-care (like meditating and exercising) while also attempting to ensure some level of privacy for them. I was so worried about missing some sign and waking up to find my child had run away in the middle of the night or had experimented and overdosed. Teens are risk takers; their behavior is often moderated by consequences of missing out on things they cherish and don't want to lose. COVID-19 took away many of those mitigating options. We all know that hopelessness coupled with fear of the unknown can create a slippery slope for teens.

I watched, listened, and comforted when I was allowed. Perhaps it was the outdoor walks that permitted clean air not filtered by a mask, the meditation cushion that I would often find one of my kids silently sitting on, or the essential oil diffuser that habitually broadcasted peace, calm, and immunity that offered those minute moments of clarity for us. Maybe it was the wine that sanctioned an interruption to my infinite worry. I am sure that a part of it was the shared laughs and the memories of their preteen years. As we eagerly await college acceptances now, I am simply grateful that we have all come out on the other side, mentally and physically stronger. Today, when faced with difficult situations, I remind myself what those COVID-19 years were like, and I am truly grateful to have lived through the pandemic. While not easy, I believe that we gained resilience, became self-care advocates, and tapped into potential that we did not know existed. I am more confident in my own abilities to navigate challenging situations and appreciate the significance of work-life balance even more now. COVID-19 was only one chapter in our story that ended just like it began—with an unconditional surplus of love and support for my now officially adult children.

Jessica Alicea-Planas PhD, RN, MPH, CHES
Mother of Alana (sixteen) and Mateo (sixteen)*
Associate Professor, Egan School of Nursing and Health Studies
*ages at the onset of the pandemic

You Can't Truly Have It All, at the Same Time

This too shall pass. Just keep doing the best you can.

—Unknown

The COVID-19 pandemic has changed all of us. What started out as something that felt like a faraway impossibility turned out to be one of the most eye-opening experiences of my lifetime. My eyes were opened to how vulnerable we really are and how valuable time really is. This time away from loved ones and experiences that we had grown to love put a spotlight on what matters most and created, for me, a mental road map for how I could get back to enjoying the simplest and most meaningful of life's joys.

During the first days and weeks of lockdown, my fear was immeasurable. The words "shelter in place" were ones I had never heard before —so much so that I had to research what this meant. Yet here we were. Told to not move. So much uncertainty and so much fear. The lockdown permeated all my senses, which triggered my already anxious personality into full-blown panic. But I have to be strong for my kids, I thought. Show them this isn't something to fear and protect them from the anxiety I felt. So, I baked (even though I am a terrible baker), and I played board games, and I told them this would be over soon and not to worry. However, kids pick up on your energy, so I am not sure how well I protected them from the fear of the everyday.

Nothing else mattered other than keeping my nuclear family safe and fed. The ridiculously long hours at work that is the norm for my career didn't seem to matter. I needed the paycheck of course, but my heart wasn't into the success of a project but the survival of my loved ones. Living in the city of Los Angeles, I would hear sirens and helicopters (which are normal parts of city life) and imagine people were dropping dead and being ushered to emergency care left and right. Was this virus living on my groceries? Was it in the air when I went to walk my dog? Could I even let my dog sniff another dog as we passed by the sidewalk, or would my dog catch it and infect my family? Is that person across the street who just coughed sick? My friendly old neighbors, whom I love, were they a biohazard threat to us now? These were my daily thoughts. Quick, hide these thoughts from the kids!

We were afraid to go to the food market, afraid to go outside. But wait, don't act like this; pretend everything is okay. Smile for the kids and show up to work every day. Be ready to put in a full day's worth of work remotely and to usher your team to deliver projects successfully while they too were in a mental spiral.

Being a working mother has never been easy. For me, I am a perfectionist. It's really hard for me to commit to something and then not give it 110 percent. Trying to find the balance of professional satisfaction while also being a present, attentive mother is a challenge on any normal day, so add in an unprecedented pandemic, and I am spinning. I would always say that when I had a successful day at work, I had failed at mothering that day and vice versa. You can't truly have it all, at the same time. The pandemic took both of my worlds and shoved it in my face twenty-four hours a day, seven days a week. There was no division of home life and work life, and the weight of having to shoulder everything at home was so very heavy. I missed my time away from the house, getting dressed up and interacting with colleagues. There were so many moments where I knew I could never have been a stay-at-home mother, and that made me feel cold and guilty. What kind of mother wants to run away?

As time went on, we adjusted. I adjusted. I found a balance that worked. I skipped my typical morning shower here and there to save that time for a relaxing bath for myself at night instead. I found when I made a little time for myself, I was calmer and more balanced for my family. I started walking the dog during conference calls. I took meetings off camera while making the first, second, or third snack of the day for the kids. I turned the stress of having no separation between work and home life into a multitasking opportunity. I've never been a fan of multitasking because I don't feel you can give your best to any one thing that way, but it is something I learned to live with and accept as a possible solution to the overwhelming feelings of having too much to do.

Although the weight of homeschooling and caring for the needs of my family all day were heavy, I also felt a silver lining was seeing my kids throughout the day. I felt that I grew to know them better; I saw them and their ability to face, for better or for worse, the day's challenges.

Then came the overwhelming guilt. How did it take a pandemic for me to see I worked too much and missed too much of my boys every day? How did I miss most evening dinners late at the office? What kind of monster was I? I love my children. I adore them. They are my world. But did I actually like my time away from the responsibilities at home? Was I absent? Could it be possible to both love the independence and successful validation my career brings me and love being a mother? Was my prior status only part-time mother for my boys? Clearly, there was a lot of internal chaos, as I found myself with the ability to now work from home but was not enjoying it.

As I write this reflection, almost two years have passed since we went into lockdown. I have come out the other side. I am no longer afraid of the virus and no longer want to be at the mercy of any one person or one thing.

It has been a difficult journey but also one of growth, both mentally and spiritually. The growth has caused me to switch companies to one that is kinder, more accepting, and allows me more flexibility to work from home whenever I need to. I have learned it is okay to prioritize my mental and physical health because if I am not well, I cannot lead the rest of my family to health. And I have accepted that it's okay to need space and enjoy time away because I have many facets to who I am, and when they are all attended too, I am better to everyone.

So, while I still believe you can't really have it all, at the same time--I now believe it's acceptable to have moments of each, whether these moments are together or separated by time and space.

I am more committed to balance, both professionally & personally. Everything truly does pass and every day, all we can do is the best we can, on that given day, in whatever space we are in.

Nicole Fina
Mother of boys six and ten*
Executive Producer
*ages at the onset of the pandemic

How the Pandemic Affected
the Tiger Mom

Intense. Competitive. Overbearing. I am a tiger mom. Yes, I said it, and I admit it. A "tiger mom," you might ask? I learned of the term "tiger mom" from Amy Chua, the author of *The Battle Hymn of the Tiger Mother*. Chua contrasts Western and Chinese parenting styles in her book. The "tiger mom" refers to the Chinese parenting style that focuses on building the child's work habits with high standards in preparation for their future. This style is in contrast to the Western parenting style, in which parents support the child's pursuit of passion and free choice. "Free choice" was what I envied among my Western friends, whom I always thought allowed to do whatever they wanted. I hung onto every word when I first read this book in my early twenties. I realized Chua was describing my childhood and upbringing. I was not alone.

I always tried to understand my upbringing with immigrant parents from China and Taiwan. I was born and raised in a small suburb in Connecticut in a predominantly white population. My parents were strict and taught me to work hard. Hard work was expected; I had no other choice. My parents grew up in Asia and immigrated to the United States (US) in their late teens and early twenties. They did not attend grade school in the US and had to adjust to American culture. They were strict, but I always equated that to their culture and language barrier. I always resented this learning curve. But as I got older, the resentment diminished when I finished graduate school, married, and had my children.

Fast forward, now it's my turn to raise my children. Before COVID-19, in 2020, they were ten and twelve. My 10-year-old daughter, Julia, was in the fourth grade, and my twelve-year-old son, Matthew, was in the sixth grade. We were overly involved in various extracurricular activities. My children were competitive swimming athletes; my son competed at the national level. Our family overbooked our schedule with swim practices, swim meets (including out-of-state meets), lacrosse practice, piano lessons, and tutor lessons.

Simultaneously, I worked as a full-time teacher and department supervisor in my school district, and my husband ran a dental practice. We were also lucky to have the help of my mother, who had recently retired. Our calendars were full, and we were always busy. I was always trying to balance work and family life, but I was obsessed with my kids and their activities.

Enter COVID-19. I started teaching and working from home while supervising the school activities of my children. Then to make the situation more stressful, my husband stopped working. His biggest fear was his profession as a dentist and his close contact with people every day because that is the only way to perform dental procedures. Is this a death sentence if he went back to practicing dentistry? Is he shut down for good? I cried myself to sleep, thinking of everything and anything that could happen to my husband.

For two weeks, we were home together as a family. For the first few days, we enjoyed this time as the kids finally had some downtime. In fact, my husband and I finally had some downtime. We all got to sleep in, relax, and venture outside to play. Then I started to panic a little inside. I was already panicking about my husband's business; now, I was panicking about my children. Then talking to another Chinese family about their situation, they were doing the same, except they had Chinese online with tutors from Wuhan, China. I quickly signed my kids up for Chinese online lessons. This tiger mom did it again. The two weeks were only a pause, but once the panic mode hit, the fear that my kids were losing time set in. I didn't want them to lose fourth and sixth grade. I was going to do everything to keep them on track. Everything moved online: school, tutoring, piano, and Chinese lessons.

My takeaway from this experience is that structure is critical not only for myself but also, and most importantly, for my children and students. Perhaps being busy is not bad after all. I believe the pandemic gave us a break and showed us how life could be without a million scheduled activities. I know I have a short time window for my children's development. The pandemic also confirmed that we need to keep moving forward, make adjustments as we go, and adapt when we can, or else we will miss the opportunities in this small window of time.

I have also learned to be flexible and adaptable to situations. If things don't go according to plan, I have learned to work through the scenario and adjust. Life will constantly be changing, and we must learn to adapt, mentally and physically. Flexibility and adaptability are what the pandemic taught me. Life is the balance of holding on and letting go.

Most importantly, I have come to appreciate my upbringing and culture. I enjoy being called a tiger mom now. It has helped my family and children navigate through the pandemic. I have learned to be strong and keep moving to support my family. As a tiger mom, this keeps me going.

Dr. Wendy A. Ku, PhD
Mother of Matthew (twelve) and Julia (ten)*
Grades seven to twelve, Career & Technical Education (CTE)
Department Supervisor/ Technology and Engineering Education
Teacher
*ages at the onset of the pandemic

Know Your Worth

Love doesn't die a natural death. It has to be killed,
either by neglect or narcissism.

—*Frank Salvato*

P re-pandemic, I was already overwhelmed with duties. I was an owner of a fledgling psychotherapy practice, an office manager and financial officer for my husband's practice, a mother of two spirited kids, an owner of a home that I mostly looked after, a chef, a bill payer, and a party thrower. The shutdown affected my son's school and husband's job, and we pulled the three-year-old from daycare to keep her safe. Now instead of just dinners, I was serving meals every two hours, teaching second grade, occupying a three-year-old nonstop, and changing bed sheets for potty-trained children, who had regressed during the shutdown. I took breaks to ugly cry in the bathroom. Sometimes, I took extra-long ugly cry breaks in the Target parking lot.

After the first two weeks, I looked at my husband, who spent time catching up on sleep and testing new bourbons from the liquor store, and fully understood why people get divorced. We discussed the effect the shutdown had on marriages worldwide. I noted that if we were living this life with the goal of retirement so that he could stay home and pick up from where he has been these past two weeks, I would not be interested in continuing this marriage. I needed help, and he was the only person available to do that. The housekeeper wasn't coming. Eating dinners out wasn't an option. The school didn't provide a relief from childcare. The snacks didn't serve themselves. The yard needed care, and he needed to be up to manage everything the one day a week I sandwiched all my patients into. He claimed everything would be okay. Apparently, that meant that nothing would change. I would continue to do all of the above while he mostly drank late and slept in.

By summer, the yard looked beautiful, second grade had ended, the three-year-old had become better at playing with her toys alone, and my husband had gone back to work. I was never the same. I always knew that in my marriage and household, I shouldered much of the burdens, but I told myself that it was because he was busy working hard and making money. Unfortunately, when given the chance to step in, he deliberately chose not to, even after my plea for help. I read many articles on marriage, parenting, division of duties, and delved into every comment section. Women from all over were discussing how divorce freed them from spouses who refused to help and worse. Better lives were possible, and being alone felt better.

The options weighed on me. I could stay married, hire the help I needed, and continue juggling all the duties. I could keep my family intact and hope that it was enough. Or I could leave the marriage and force a division of not only labor but also kids, office, and life. I am not the type of person who forces or pushes situations into my favor. But I had forced myself into roles that my husband and I had openly discussed would be egalitarian when we chose to marry. Worst of all, my children saw it. My son told his aunt that he wanted a kid one day, so he could play catch with him. He then told her that he would need a wife to do everything else. My daughter would check on me at the bathroom door, ready with hugs and pictures to make me feel better. If I stayed, I would be endorsing this type of marriage to them. If I stayed, I'd be the worst type of parent—the one that set my children up for future failed marriages with unrealistic expectations of their spouse or themselves. I would be saying: "Shrink to fit in your marriage, dear girl. Get your wife to handle it all, sweet boy." Consequences.

Ironically, a year synonymous with perfect vision, I saw my life perfectly. Every lie I told to keep the status quo palatable for myself over the years fell away, and only the ugly truth was left. With shaky hands and a lot of heartache, I filed for divorce in August of 2020.

Anonymous, PhD
Mother of two kids
Clinical Psychologist

Post-COVID Self

There was Pre-COVID me, and now there is this me.

— *Anna Paskausky*

It's late March 2020, and I'm standing in my living room giving three shots to each of my preemie twins; COVID-19 may have kept me out of the office for a two-month checkup, but I wasn't going to get off the vaccination schedule. I'm a nurse practitioner, PhD prepared. I saw the cluster of evidence before March that told me the virus was going to blow up all my carefully laid plans: childcare, the parade of aunties holding the babies so I could shower, visits with family, nights off with friends at the brewery, progress on work projects, writing, and getting in better shape. LOL. Not to be.

The pandemic is like the K-T boundary (the geologic evidence around the world of the mass extinction event that killed the dinosaurs). There was pre-COVID me, and now there is this me. Like the dinosaurs, part of me died those long months in the dark of the pandemic, with two tiny premature babies (one a NICU graduate) and an energetic and anxious three-year-old and working remotely doing telehealth when my leave ended. We were alone, essentially, or alone enough for the pre-COVID me, accounting for American standards appropriate to my class and station.

Professionally, I came to love telehealth. I was diagnosing stroke, diverticulitis, and polymyalgia rheumatica and treating depression, so much depression, anxiety, fatigue, and malaise. In those countless telehealth appointments, I realized what I already knew as a nurse: The patient story (or their medical history) is usually the key element that drives the medical decision-making process. This process is Prometheus's fire, as it transforms me from a nurse to a nurse practitioner that can bill and diagnose and treat diseases. It was satisfying to feel more connected to the nursing part of being a nurse practitioner, even as I worked in isolation at home in between my family.

I worked out of bathrooms and bedrooms—nothing a screen, lighting, crisp shirt collars, and noise reduction couldn't overcome. I only stopped a visit twice for my kids: once upon hearing the sickening thud of a head hitting the floor and once when I forgot to lock the door, and my preschooler wanted to tell me something.

Personally, I don't have a thesis of insight. I haven't had time to reflect, to process, to make meaning of these relentless, gruelling two years because my pandemic isn't over. My telehealth days have flipped into a full-time clinic, with the mask-goggle lines and the thin protection of a cotton-poly blend white coat. I'm more than two full-time equivalents (FTE) between my childcare duties and my job taking care of other people. Someday, I will have insight. Someday, I will understand in context. But for now, it's enough for me to know the pre-COVID me is gone, and her ambitions, illusions, and ideals do not apply. The scale has changed, and the playing field has collapsed. The song changed mid-tune on my one turn at the karaoke mic.

I hope that all the other mothers out there—especially my healthcare colleagues who have been bruised, battered, and betrayed by the man-made systems we altruistically work in—will tell the truth: This isn't working. Our pre-COVID selves never spoke up: too polite, infinitely able to adjust, to compensate, and to take on more. Now, our post-COVID selves are depleted, straightforward, and fiercely protective (of our patients, ourselves, and our families) and have so much less to lose. Can we demand a work life balance that works? You bet we can. Can we keep the healthcare ship afloat until we make it less terrible and dehumanizing—absolutely. The system must change because we have changed.

It would be unwise to test us and to wave smoke and mirror spreadsheets and recite market value incantations to restore the way it was. The dinosaur's disaster gave way to the rise of the mammals, so mamas, let's evolve.

Anna Paskausky, PhD, MS, RN, CNP, FNP-BC
Mother of Cedar (three), Remedy (one month), and Lark (one month)*
Advanced Practitioner Supervisor Primary Care, Nurse Practitioner
*ages at the onset of the pandemic

Pandemic Hardship

Even when we can't control the situation around us,
we always can choose where we're directing our attention.

—*Elizabeth Stanley*

Our working lives have been changing for some time, but the emergence of the COVID-19 pandemic has led to a massive shift, more uncertainty, and new challenges for many of us. As a small business owner who faced months of a lockdown, inaccessible supplies/products, and a world of new regulations and guidelines, mental health concerns became unavoidable for me. All the while, I was also worrying and considering what my clients' comfort levels would be when returning for hair services after the lockdown. Who would be willing to stay with me considering these new circumstances? Would clients who had begun coloring their own hair at home no longer require that service? Could my clients afford price changes I had to make? How would they feel once inside the salon with other people there? The questions in my head were countless. There were numerous conflicts and situations that could alter the dynamics of my salon, and I wasn't sure whether I'd be able to survive the pandemic. Was this the end of my time at the salon?

Returning to work with all of the new regulations and challenges was difficult to say the least; the hair color supply I needed was prohibitively expensive, when it was available. The majority of the items I need to work are imported from other countries, and with factories closing and people being laid off, receiving these items has become increasingly difficult. The price of these items has also nearly quadrupled, putting stylists out of work or unable to keep up financially. Some people were relieved when the government offered unemployment to those who were self-employed for the first time, but I was unable to receive this assistance due to taxes and what I made the year prior. Applying for small business loans, paycheck protection program loans, as well as other loans through color firms revealed that obtaining a small business loan was more difficult than in past years, owing to the pandemic. Everyone around me who ran a business (not just salon-related businesses) seemed to be receiving either a loan or unemployment benefits. Everything I had fought so hard for appeared to be flashing before my eyes. When is this going to be over? What would I do if I couldn't do hair?

Throughout this time and the changes it brought, my mental health started to unravel. To add to the commotion, Carley and Elliana's school was closed in March 2020, and it wouldn't reopen until September. I decided to keep them on a distance learning program (even when things reopened) due to Elliana's underlying health issues, which prevent her from receiving vaccinations. Trying to maintain routine, while dealing with new technology, was difficult for all of us, especially when technology isn't my strong suit. As the pressures and stressful situations mounted, I realized we needed to begin by accepting the uncertainties.

I started to feel as though my mental health was at risk, and regardless of our individual situations, the COVID-19 outbreak had, and will forever have, a significant impact on how we think, feel, and respect ourselves and the world we live in. In the beginning, as a result of the pandemic, my family's weekly schedules and routines shifted. I quickly realized for my children's wellbeing that all electronic time, including online schooling, needed to be limited or altered. I made breaks for both girls and went back to "old school," as my daughters would say. Home economics, outdoor recreation, and arts and crafts were among some of the changes I made. I made adjusted measurements for my girls when cooking and baking to require extra thought and arithmetic abilities. The baked goods were sent to relatives and friends who we could only see through doors or windows. But we could still express our love and support through freshly baked items. Being outside became a huge change in a way I hadn't anticipated. We had always liked the outdoors as a family—hiking, bicycling, fishing, beaching, gardening, and so on—but the kids were now learning new skills. Elliana mastered riding her bike without training wheels, allowing us to all travel trails together. In the driveway, we were playing with chalk and putting our artistic abilities to the test. They even learned how to play real hopscotch, despite Carley's assertion that simply hopping is the proper method. I'd make up these scavenger hunt games with all kinds of stuff the kids had to find that contained particular letters or had certain meanings. Every Wednesday and Friday, the girls had to decide on a theme night as a family. Whether it was ice cream sundae night, movie night, or game night, everyone had a good time. Using goods that we already possessed and changing their appearance to meet our themes were astonishing. We would try to learn something new about one another or work on something we wanted to work on during our theme nights.

All of these new approaches drew us closer together, and I began to observe a significant difference in all of our attitudes, habits, and even perspectives on certain topics. It's amazing to see how much my daughters have grown as well as how brilliant and creative they are. We were all striving as a family to keep our thoughts and brains moving forward in the hopes of resuming routine. Part of me didn't want it to be normal, since I was loving the new lifestyle we had created. The reality of the pandemic, with our stay-at-home orders and changes in our working environment, had its ups and downs, but it ultimately taught us many things as a family and as individuals. Family fun nights didn't have to be store bought, but rather could be invented at home with what we already owned; showing love to extended family and friends came through the joys of sharing a fresh batch of chocolate chip cookies and ultimately being outdoors together with no agenda other than to simply be. This drew us closer and stronger as individuals and as a family. The lessons taught, the memories we made, and the perspectives my daughters and I held onto for dealing with and respecting others in good or bad situations, or even those somewhere in the middle, had at their core the values of family and love.

Jeana Wallace
Mother of Carley (twelve) and Elliana (seven)*
Hairstylist and Owner of Autumn Rae Salon
*ages at the onset of the pandemic

Stressed Out

If stress burned calories, I'd be a supermodel.

—Unknown

Stress. Stress is a normal part of my job and daily life. Everyday there are varying levels of stress to deal with, and because of this, I have developed a tolerance to it (or at least I seem to think I have). So, at the beginning of 2020 when I was reassigned to a different position in my job, school resource officer, I thought to myself here's my break. Here's my escape from all the stress. My schedule was about to become a normal nine to five. I would work Monday through Fridays and have my weekends off. Weekends off meant I could coach my daughter's soccer teams and attend all their games and never miss birthday parties or dinners with family and friends. Working at the school also meant I was no longer going to have to work out on the highways on patrol. It meant, in some crazy way, I was out of harm's way a lot more often than I was going to be in it. My job just got a little safer. My stress level would be greatly reduced. The year appeared as though it was going to be a good one for me, or so I thought.

I was approximately one month into my new assignment, just starting to feel comfortable, when talks of a mystery virus originating in China began to emerge. The rumors and whisperings of schools closing for two weeks continued for the next week or so before an official announcement was made. The high school I was assigned to would be shutting down for at least two weeks, but deep down I knew we would not be reopening in two weeks. I was mad, the position I had always wanted was being ripped away from me by some virus, and there was nothing I could do about it. I also knew it meant gone were my days of working a normal nine to five, I would have to go back to a rotational work schedule (work five days and get three days off). My stress level was going up.

So much was unknown about COVID-19 at the time. No one really knew how easily it spread or how severe it would be. Whereas most working parents were slowly being told to work from home to avoid contact with others in the office, I did not have this luxury. I had to go to work every day and possibly expose myself to COVID-19. I was sent out to do my job with extremely limited PPE, one N95 mask and five surgical masks. We were all reusing the same PPE for weeks on end. My husband, Kevin, is a paramedic/firefighter who, at the time, worked two jobs, both of which involved riding in an ambulance with patients who potentially had COVID-19.

At the time this occurred, my oldest daughter, Madelyn (Maddie), was in first grade and now had to do remote learning from home. My other daughter, Samantha (Sammie), was enrolled in a small in-home daycare. Even though her daycare remained open, Kevin and I had to decide whether we would send her there every day. Due to Kevin and my possible exposure to COVID-19 on a regular basis, we decided to keep Sammie home. We did not want to potentially expose other families at the daycare to COVID-19. At this point, we were left with two young children at home and two parents that had to report to work. We needed to find some type of childcare.

We live within fifteen minutes of my parents and thankfully they are both retired, so it was an easy solution, right? In normal circumstances, the answer would be yes! They are our go-to childcare option on a regular basis, and we are forever grateful. However, when you take into consideration my father's medical history, he was quickly classified as high risk. My mother, though overall healthy, also had a medical condition that rendered her higher risk. So now I had my two parents who were high risk and literally no other option for childcare. So, at least two to three times a week (when my husband and my schedules overlapped), we had to have my mother watch our children. I felt as though I was risking both of my parents' lives every time I went to work but like many first responders, we were out of options. A temporary, special family medical leave law the state of Connecticut put into place specifically did not allow for first responders or medical care workers to use it. It felt like a slap in the face, and I was beginning to feel high levels of stress.

While at work, I tried to have the least amount of exposure to other people as possible, and at home, we were surviving the pandemic the best we could. I never realized how much time was taken up by sports, birthday parties, and family outings until the whole world shut down. In the beginning, we managed to build our kids a treehouse with all our extra free time. We got into a routine with all the remote learning, and it felt as though things would be okay. I was feeling slightly less stressed and overwhelmed, but then May 25 occurred.

I will only mention the following incident once because it was so horrible, but it must be mentioned because it greatly affected my personal pandemic experience. George Floyd's death at the hands of deplorable police officers occurred on May 25, causing a nationwide movement of advocating for the defunding of law enforcement. Within a week of this incident, I was forced to work fifteen-hour days, two days in a row, and in two different cities because of protesters blocking state highways. I was rerouted countless times during my regular shifts to various highways for the same reason. The things yelled at me and my fellow law enforcement officers at those protests were horrendous. I must say not all protesters were the same, and I had meaningful conversations with some of them, but overall, the mood of the protesters was not in support of police officers.

Things changed drastically for me at this time. I left my house every morning (we drive our patrol cars home in my state) thinking I could be ambushed in my driveway. My fellow troopers felt the same way. Every hair on my body would rise if a car drove up next to me in a parking lot. Does this person want to harm me? Do they have a gun? I was anxious and paranoid during my shifts, never knowing if someone wished me harm for just being a law enforcement officer. I stopped driving my patrol car with my children in it for fear someone may try to kill me and they hurt them as well. My profession was under attack, and I felt like I had to defend myself to everyone I met, even those people who had known me my whole life. I was called all sorts of names. It was exhausting and emotionally draining. I was experiencing extremely high levels of stress and had to find an outlet. I felt like the pandemic was finally starting to break me. I needed to get my sanity back. I needed a break.

I love to travel. Traveling helps me escape my real life for a short period of time. COVID-19 was making travel difficult. I was determined, however, to not let it ruin my entire year, and thankfully my family loves camping. Camping seemed to be a COVID-19 friendly vacation option.

Since we own a camper, our family already had six trips planned for 2020. Our first one (Memorial Day weekend) was cancelled, but my husband and I vowed to go on all our other camping trips. In our opinion, it was a relatively safe way to vacation. My family and my extended family go on a large group vacation every year as well, and we all vowed to still go on vacation if everyone was feeling well. To be honest, we had all been seeing each other the whole time anyway so we were really one large pod. These escapes from work and reality were exactly what my mind and body needed. We did everything as safely as possible; we always wore masks and followed the rules, but I could not let COVID-19 take everything away from me. I know my choice might not have been the most popular, as many people did not travel at all during the pandemic, but it was the necessary choice for me and my mental health. I was carefree while away; no one knew who I was or what I did for work. I was able to escape my reality for a moment.

I learned a lot from pandemic life. It showed me how much I love family time and how much fun we can have without all the crazy distractions of normal everyday life. I learned that time with my family and time spent away from my job could be healing. I was beyond stressed for most of 2020. I know it wasn't healthy. I know fellow law-enforcement officers that had mental breakdowns, and I also spent some days and nights crying from the stress, but I feel like I came out stronger. I know I grew emotionally and learned that I am stronger than I thought. Pandemic life reiterated for me how we are all different people. Even though my friends or family chose to do things differently than myself, we can all respect one another's opinions and boundaries. Everyone had different reasons for how they chose to survive the pandemic and I learned to respect that.

I also learned that spending every minute off from work with my husband and kids can be extremely difficult. There were many rocky moments (trust me), but in the end, I developed a greater appreciation for my husband and for my kids and how well they could make me feel whole again after really terrible days. We came out stronger as a family unit. We survived.

Jennifer Yokley
Mother of Madelyn (six) and Samantha (four)*
Detective, Connecticut State Police
*ages at the onset of the pandemic

Discussion

Adiamond stone, in all its shining grandeur, is produced only under immense pressure, at intense heat. One can easily say the intensity of a global pandemic brought pressures for women that were at times insurmountable, and throughout it all, personal growth emerged amid a world full of relentless demands from home and work. At a time when knowledge related to the pandemic was scarce, these women's worries centered on protecting themselves and their families, managing schooling/childcare, and maintaining wage earning careers. This was a period of intense pressure and heat, yet their boldest selves were revealed because of the demands they faced. Through the constant noise and chaos of the pandemic, the women in these narratives utilized this pressure to consistently foster growth in themselves and for their families—a growth that only occurred because of the trials presented in working and mothering during this time. The sharing of their growth does not negate the challenges of the pandemic. It is through facing, naming, and consciously working through the difficulties, they are in the place they are—on the other side stronger as individuals and as mothers.

One of the most tangible similarities is childbirth. When giving birth, mothers must work through all of the sensations and emotions associated with labor. They must literally push through physical discomfort to arrive at the moment of reaching down and welcoming their newborn into their hands. The only way to that moment is to push through and to persevere. As these women in this chapter have displayed, being present with the pandemic discomfort and working through it were the catalyst for growth.

These women also show us how having grit provides a pivotal launch point for this growth. Grit is the passion and persistence for seeing one's goals through despite all odds (Duckworth). Gritty people aren't immune to the highs and the lows, but rather have a tenacity and passion to see their projects through any obstacles that present (Duckworth). To think more deeply about this concept of grit, you can picture a flower blooming through the cracks of a concrete sidewalk. When despite all obstacles, the seed germinated, water made its way to the roots, and sunlight found it so that it was able to bloom in all its vibrant glory. Was this sidewalk the location the flower wanted to grow in? We would argue no; it wasn't ideal. These women would say that the pandemic wasn't their chosen way to find this growth. But when the situation presented itself, they too rose, revealing their true vibrancy.

As Jen, a state detective and mother of two, recounted, she lacked childcare options, and there were immense changes to her profession. She openly shared grappling with high levels of stress and exhaustion; she reached a breaking point. When she realized she was drained, she found the outlet of camping with family—something that COVID-19 hadn't taken away or upended and that provided the necessary reset. Ultimately, she wrote: "I feel like I came out stronger. I know I grew emotionally and learned that I am stronger than I thought." Similarly, Jeanna, a hairstylist and small business owner with two daughters, accepted the uncertainties and grew as a result. All the work she had done for her family and her business was upended by the pandemic, and in that moment, she openly said that her mental health started to "unravel." It was through "accepting the uncertainties," intentionally spending time in nature, playing games as a family, and baking that her family grew closer. Holding "family and love" central during this time allowed for her growth. Importantly, these women displayed emotional regulation, which can bolster wellbeing (Di Blasi 9).

Alongside this regulation, the trait of grit was noticed in each of these women's experiences. Angela Duckworth, mother and career woman herself, has published and spoken extensively on the concept of grit. Research done early on in the pandemic (spring 2020) has shown that individuals who had children living at home and who moved their body through any form of physical activity demonstrated higher grit scores during the pandemic (Totosy de Zepetnek 3). Additionally, higher grit during the pandemic was found in those who had a more intense mental workload on workdays, suggesting that wage-earning individuals like these mothers display more grit (Totosy de Zepetnek 4). Wendy, a district level school administrator and technology educator, demonstrated grit through her steadfastness to maintain the standards and values of her Chinese upbringing amid the chaos and disruption of the pandemic. Her relentless priority to ensure high educational standards for her children, a value that has been passed on to her from her immigrant parents, was as unfaltering as her discovery that this inherited grit delivered her through hardship and affirmed her strength. As she said, "The pandemic also confirmed that we need to keep moving forward... and we must learn to adapt, mentally and physically."

Resilience also plays a role in positively mediating stress (Demetrio 54; Kumar et al. 144) as was seen in these gritty mothers. For Jessica, a university associate professor and mom of twin teenagers, she too recounted the humbling realities that came with maintaining a career while mothering during a pandemic. Through it all, she relied on honoring her emotions first, meditating, using essential oils, and taking outdoor walks, which all provided "moments of clarity." She is not alone, as other mothers working in academia have revealed not only the countless struggles but also the moments of joy they found in their pandemic situations (Hayden and O'Brien Hallstein 170, 176). Jessica is "grateful to come out on the other side mentally and physically stronger." "COVID-19 was only one chapter" in her story.

Similarly, Nicole, an executive producer and a mother of two, said: "It is okay to prioritize my mental and physical health... I have many facets of who I am, and when they are all attended to, I am better to everyone." Through her pandemic experience, she realized "you can't truly have it all, at the same time." While appreciating time with her boys, she realized she also finds connection and validation in her career. To support and honor both of these parts of who she is, she used this growth as a catalyst and found a more flexible company to work for.

Because of the pandemic, these women, and countless others, were caught between a rock and a hard place. And from this place of upheaval, they named and owned the experience. They slowly rose from the exhaustion, depression, fear, and despair, to say: I can do this. I am here. I am standing. I am stronger.

For some women, being stronger meant shedding what no longer served them. A clinical psychologist and a mom of two saw her life with "perfect vision" and clarity during the pandemic. She shed a marriage that no longer served her, and in doing so, she showed her children that she was advocating for a world of equality in gender roles. She assured her daughter didn't learn to "shrink to fit" into a future marriage and that her son didn't think he could get his future wife to "handle" all of the domestic responsibilities. The pandemic gave her the clarity to be the strong, brave, and inspiring mother she wants her kids to see, to love, and to learn from. And Anna, a mother of three and a nurse practitioner supervisor, has clearly shed her former self. With the pandemic, "the scale has changed, and the playing field has collapsed. The song changed mid-tune." She let go of what was and is no longer the same career mother. She has shed her pre-COVID self because life in that space quite simply "wasn't working." Through her evolution, she is also encouraging mothers everywhere to rise up and do the same—to demand better work-life boundaries.

Steps to Re-imagining

Active work is needed to get to the other side of a hardship. The mothers in this chapter did not fight against the world's pandemic upheaval; instead, they fought for themselves to come out stronger—a truly inspiring and bold insight.

When we are not sure what's coming next, it may seem easiest to just turn the other way, but these women's narratives and insights remind us that facing adversity and the unknowns with grit can lead to positive change. The discomforts of the pandemic were certainly not welcome ones, but because of these events, the insights these women revealed were mental and physical growth; they became stronger in ways only the pandemic and its adversity could have prompted. They did not hide their truths. We must travel through the darkness to see our light (L'Engle). There is no clarity without both.

One's true potential is released not in the easy moments but through the ones fraught with hardship and struggle. The pandemic brought with it momentous hurdles and placed them directly in front of mothers, who were both caring for their children and working. None of these mothers' accounts are offered through rose-colored lenses. In fact, they each named the struggles that occurred for them personally and professionally. Major life changes—such as divorce, leaving a job, and wondering if a hair salon would pull through following the pandemic lockdown—were their realities. Through it all, perseverance and grit were championed by these women, thus allowing their growth as mothers and career women to emerge. Growth surfaced through the active work of honoring both pleasant and unpleasant feelings and deeply reflecting on them with friends, family, or a mental health provider—and for some, by simply reflecting in their own personal way. These women took off the mask of having it all together and showed that pandemic life was messy, emotionally challenging, and relentlessly brutal. Their growth came only with sitting in the uncomfortable moments.

Reflective Prompts

1. Difficulty can be a catalyst for thriving mentally and physically and also an opportunity to reframe personal and professional successes. How might you evaluate your pandemic experience to see the places you have grown?

2. Since the onset of the pandemic, can you share what in your personal and professional life has changed? Are you the same mother, person, and colleague?

3. Can you share an example of a time you demonstrated grit? How can you cultivate grit in yourself? Make a list of at least three ways you can start to dig in and show your grit.

4. What do you hope to develop or to cultivate in yourself personally over the next three months? In the next year? In the next five years?

Works Cited

Chua, Amy. *The Battle Hymn of the Tiger Mother.* Penguin Press, 2011.

Di Blasi, Maria, et al. "Factors Related to Women's Psychological Distress during the COVID-19 Pandemic: Evidence from a Two-Wave Longitudinal Study." *International Journal of Environmental Research and Public Health,* vol. 18, 6 Nov. 2021, pp. 1-12.

Demetrio, Loukia. "The Impact of the Covid-19 Lockdown Measures on Mental Health and Well-Being and the Role of Resilience: A

Review of Studies in Cyprus." *IOSR Journal of Humanities and Social Science*, vol. 26, no. 4, 2021, pp. 54-65.

Duckworth, Angela. *Grit: The Power of Passion and Perseverance*. Scribner, 2016.

Hayden, Sara, and Lynn O'Brien Hallstein. "An Ode to Academic Mothers: Finding Gratitude and Grace in the Midst of COVID-19." *Mothers, Mothering, and COVID-19: Dispatches from the Pandemic*, edited by Andrea O'Reilly and Fiona Joy Green, Demeter Press, 2021, pp. 169-80.

Kumar, Shivani, et al. "Resilience: A Mediator of the Negative Effects of Pandemic-Related Stress on Women's Mental Health in the USA." *Archives of Women's Mental Health*, vol. 25, 2022, pp. 137-46.

L'Engle, Madeleine. *A Ring of Endless Light*. Crosswicks, Ltd, 1980.

Stanley, Elizabeth. *Widen the Window: Training Your Brain and Body to Thrive During Stress and Recover from Trauma*. Avery, 2019.

Tedeschi, Richard G., and Lawrence G. Calhoun. "Posttraumatic Growth: Conceptual Foundations and Empirical Evidence." *Psychological Inquiry*, vol. 15, no. 1, pp. 1-18.

Totosy de Zepetnek, J. O., et al. "Influence of Grit on Lifestyle Factors During the COVID-19 Pandemic in a Sample of Adults in the United States." *Personality and Individual Differences*, vol. 175, 2021, pp. 1-7.

Chapter 8

Unveiling Agency

*The task is not to control the wind, but to direct
the movements of the ship so that it stays its course.*

—*Unknown*

One of the most sobering aspects of the pandemic, particularly early on, was the displacement of many relative constants—the physical workplace, the social itinerary, as well as one's general sense of psychological and physical safety. For many, the displacement brought to light both an eroding sense of control over the familiar and a steady intrusion of the elusive. The following collection of essays depicts narratives of how such displacement inspired these mothers with the insights and opportunity on how to rework their mental frameworks governing control. These seven mothers had children ranging from ages two to fifteen at the start of the pandemic and maintained careers spanning the following industries: corporate marketing, pharmaceuticals, health/nutrition, and academia. Each one shares how navigating their career and home responsibilities inspired them to seize unfolding opportunities.

Of Plagues and Poetry

What we have lived
Remains indecipherable.
& yet we remain.
& still, we write.
Watch us move above the fog
Like a promontory at dusk.
Shall this leave us bitter?
Or better?

Grieve.

Then choose.

—Amanda Gorman

Any experience is given meaning and color by the timeframe we put around it, particularly the end point from which we choose to look back and reflect with some sense approaching finality or culmination. It was not until my family and me were finally hit by COVID-19, had recovered our health, looked furtively around, and decided it was safe to take our masks off, to try to live life again, that I felt truly able to understand and articulate my experience of the pandemic over the last two and a half years. We had survived it. Within our family circles, major tragedy had been averted. Barring any new and more dangerous variants, it appears that we are emerging into a post-COVID-19 world and shedding the paralyzing fear, isolation, and painful caution that had governed and restricted our lives. It is the moment I can make some sense of what has happened—to process the fact that I stand here in the summer of 2022 as something more than simply a traumatized survivor. Is it possible that although the living nightmare had appeared to raze the very ground I stood on, strong green shoots now appear to push up through the scarred surface? How is it that our lives in some ways were devastated, chaotic, stalled, and stagnant and in others focussed, serene, meaningful, and even thriving? I reflect here on the nature of the jolt that the COVID-19 pandemic had on my life as a mother, scholar, wife, and human being. I am sure that this is just the beginning of making out its meaning.

Yet there were moments along the way that served as markers, places where we paused and processed. In June 2020, my husband and I sat down for an interview on an Ancient Faith podcast geared to our Greek Orthodox community. He was asked to describe his experience as a medical professional on the front lines of the COVID-19 war. We recounted our family's proactive quarantine and separation during the first, most terrifying wave. I spoke of the necessity of essentially home-schooling the children. We both reflected on how our faith—bolstered by virtual church, online prayer groups, and tales of the miracles of Saint Nikiforos—got us through a dark time. After the interview was over, we looked at each other and cried. I'm not sure we'd ever done that; I don't think any life experience had ever levelled us emotionally in that way. We felt a weight had lifted and experienced some relief. We naively thought we had made it through the worst of it. But there was so much more endurance required, so much more terror ahead.

Eventually, I halted my scholarly work almost entirely, and my momentum and the mental clarity required to research and write are only just getting back. I began the pandemic lockdown with wonderful intentions of reading scholarship and primary texts as the kids were occupied with math exercises or playing games together at a common "recess" time, and trying to write a little every evening after tucking them into bed. I was going to parent all day in total isolation, teach a first grader to read, grapple with a fourth grader's writing disability, get through the numbing fear that my husband could contract COVID-19 in the ER from a patient at any time and die, and continue to write original and informed ideas about maternal protagonists in the British novel. That plan quickly became untenable.

As soul sustaining and as important as the work was and continues to be, both personally and professionally, in the pandemic environment of uncertainty and fear, I chose some form of self-preservation. For me, it meant letting slide the deadline I had control over, focussing on shedding preventable stresses and maintaining some normalcy in our home. I chose to find joy in the quiet moments with my children, my main companions. I marvelled as they netted frogs in the spring and cheered them on as they rode up and down the driveway trying to catch spiralling leaves in the fall. I opened up my home office door for frequent interruptions when one had a snack break and wanted company and another needed emotional and academic support to draft a writing piece on dinosaurs. The children were home for an entire year—the first few months because everything was shut down and then the next several because we chose a remote school option. We were not letting COVID-19 slip in through any cracks. My husband posed a tremendous risk to our household that we could not fully mitigate; we decided that the kids staying home meant we were sealed pretty tightly.

Before I had temporarily paused my work, I was rereading Elizabeth Gaskell's *Ruth* and was mystified and haunted by its description of an epidemic of illness in the countryside, which hadn't even resonated with me in my first (pre-pandemic) encounter with the text. I was writing a dissertation chapter on "model mothers"—about two maternal protagonists each parenting in (relative) isolation, mothering through stressful personal circumstances, and prioritizing the wellbeing of their children. It was a chapter I wanted to celebrate in that I was finally looking at healthy maternal subjects, also at the center of the stories, after tracing, in my research, so many featured neglectful and scheming mothers. Not only were Helen Huntingdon and Ruth Hilton good mothers, but they also, as I argue in my chapter, ultimately experience an activation of their talents and even an awakening of vocation partly due to the demands of their particular personal circumstances (that is, the need to craftily use their resources to survive) and also due to their mothering. As I often do, I felt the books were speaking to me, offering a unique comfort and a feeling of hope in the most lonely and frightening period of my life. I thought of the determination and bravery of the saintly Ruth, giving her life to heal others from sickness and ultimately losing her own. She was in my mind as I watched my husband put on his scrubs each day and leave to treat COVID-19 patients or manage the reworking of an emergency department to meet new pandemic demands. I considered the artistry of Helen Huntingdon, churning out paintings for money to sustain herself and her son, and I thought of how she sharpened her skills responding to grinding need. As I wrote about Helen Huntingdon and Ruth Hilton in the evenings, fighting off fatigue, they inspired and invigorated me. Here were two women, albeit fictional, passing through some version of personal hell, creating environments of nurture and safety for their sons, and, through their trials, arriving at capable and blooming versions of themselves. I didn't dare think it was possible for me. I prayed for survival, just a chance, to be around for my children, family, and friends and to continue the work I felt uniquely fitted for.

As I consider now, perhaps I did more than survive. Like Helen and Ruth, my instinct to provide some emotional buffer for my children from the horrors around us helped to bond us uniquely and left them with some sense of safety and even delight in our time together at home. I take pride in that. Like Helen and Ruth, I sharpened some skills that will serve me in the future: the ability to change and alter ingrained life patterns, the discerning of what is nonessential, the unearthing of the deep knowledge of who I really am in a most destitute and raw form, and also the instinct for what I need to nourish myself and what I feel called upon to give in this world. Those things felt obvious during the pandemic. They were so evident that they were visceral. After a collective brush with death, a glimpse at apocalypse, I pared down life to what mattered: the need for global cooperation to preserve humanity and our earth and our individual dedication to our various callings and gifts. I was so thankful for those, like my husband, who were called upon to serve the sick. I could never have done it. Instead, I was drawn into my books. I taught virtually, feeling the sacredness in connecting to my students in an environment of insecurity and fear. And I wrote more poetry than I ever have before, often in bed, often in the dark on a virtual notepad, attempting to shape the chaos the pandemic brought to our lives.

I marvel that it is poetry that came to me so instinctually, not narrative and novel as I had studied, not the academic work I was supposed to be writing. It came as both deeply personal comfort and global commentary, insisting upon itself, the words filling the silences in my mind. Today domestic life and the professional feel more organically woven together in this way, even as the abrupt pandemic collision of those worlds subsides.

I can boast of no PhD diploma earned, no book published, not even an academic job begun. In many ways, the pandemic brought me back to the professional paralysis of stay-at-home motherhood that I had been slowly breaking. However, I remembered how scholarly work and writing had been possible once, with supports in place, and I knew it would be possible, perhaps even better, again.

Anastasia Vahaviolos Valassis
Mother of Alex (nine) and Maddie (six)*
PhD Candidate in English Literature
Graduate Center, CUNY
*ages at the onset of the pandemic

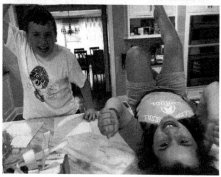

The World We Create

*I am prouder of my years as a single mother
than of any other part of my life.*
—*JK Rowling*

I haven't touched a doorknob in at least five years or shaken anyone's hand. I don't ever touch the poles on subways or buses or the railings on stairs or escalators. Doctors' offices? Forget it.

By March 7, 2020, my basement looked like a bunker: I had been buying antibacterial supplies and preparing for this pandemic for weeks, well before the virus hit the United States (US). It seemed as if no one else was taking the news seriously, but this anxious germaphobe and hypochondriac was.

As a germ freak, I had been training for this pandemic my entire adult life. I was prepared to take on the germs and protect my children from them. What I wasn't prepared for was the tremendous weight I felt as a single parent to create a life in quarantine for my twelve- and four-teen-year-old children while holding down a full-time job. I'll never forget the day they came home from their last day of school in March 2020; they looked at me and said gleefully: "What are we doing now?"

The weight of this question hit me like a brick. What ARE we doing now? What will my children do now, and how will I make whatever that happen while working? Although the kids' school had been shut down indefinitely, little in my work world had shut down. On the contrary, my work as a faculty developer ramped up exponentially, as it became clear that our faculty development office needed to prepare and support hundreds of full- and part-time faculty to teach online, almost immediately. I was soon staffing a faculty help desk from 8:00 a.m. to 8:00 p.m. while my children were in the background of my Zoom camera making every baked good known to humankind.

I knew that for me to have any chance at doing my job, my children needed some structure. The teacher in me created a weekly schedule that required my kids to spend an hour each day doing something academic, something aerobic, and something for the good of the household. By some miracle (and a few incentives), they bought into this daily schedule for ten weeks (still shocked), which was enough to get me through the end of the semester. In hindsight, I think they were looking for something to hold onto as much as I was—some structure, some accountability, and some normalcy—as they checked off their jobs each day. Since I worked from our dining room table, there were no boundaries between living, working, parenting, and adulting. They all blurred together in my Zoom meetings, where my kids entered in and out my classes and workshops as in a reality TV show. No question—apparently—was inappropriate to ask me while I was actively teaching or leading a workshop (Christian: Is tuberculosis contagious?), despite my daily pleas to only interrupt my classes for emergencies. (Apparently, being out of bread flour is an emergency.) There was no alone time. Ever.

I remember sitting with my children at dinner one night while they bemoaned the prospect of yet another week in quarantine. At that moment, I shared a mantra I had been feeling inside: "You're not going to get this time back." They wouldn't get their seventh, eighth, ninth, or tenth grades back. They wouldn't get their birthdays back, their sports seasons, or their summers. We needed to embrace this unusual time and make the best of it. A mom interviewed by NPR put it well: "What can we do right now to make this moment something?"

So, we did. We made it something. Much to their chagrin, I took my children on a hike or outing every weekend—the beach, the woods, the neighborhood. We discovered hikes and parks I didn't even know existed within a few miles of our home. I taught my son how to drive. I dusted off my 1995 rollerblades and went skating with my daughter in the empty school parking lot every day during my lunch break. Our dog got 1,432 walks. We did crafts and redid bedrooms. We had Thanksgiving alone, just the three of us, for the first time in my life. It was amazing. Together, we created a modified world that filled our days and minds with enough structure and meaning to feel okay. It wasn't always pretty (I went on a cooking strike for a week in early fall 2020), but it worked. And despite the heaviness of the time, the loneliness of both too much and too little human contact, I'm so very grateful for this uninterrupted time I had with my children to connect and find our way, a new way, to be together.

My greatest insight from mothering and working during the pandemic is that my children's world is the world I create for them, not simply the world that is thrown our way—be it a pandemic, a terminal cancer diagnosis, or a broken heart. I say this knowing I enjoyed great privilege during this time. I could work from the safety of my home. I could care for my children in between (and during) meetings and classes. My children were largely self-sufficient, and I had the financial resources to have food and supplies delivered to my home. And so, we persisted in this pandemic and world being grateful for the privileges we have as a family of three and conscious of the agency we have to create a world full of meaning, whatever the challenges that come our way.

I conclude with my daughter's eternal optimism, who said every night at dinner (no matter how terrible my cooking was): this is the best meal of the pandemic. Because it was.

Emily R. Smith, PhD
*Mother of Christian (fifteen) and Carly (thirteen)**
Professor of English Education, Director of Mentoring
*ages at the outset of the pandemic

Where She Is
Supposed to Be...

And we know that all things work together for good to them that love God,
to them who are the called according to his purpose.
—Holy Bible, Romans 8:28

April 1, 2020, I began my first day as an executive of a healthcare company. I was thirty-three years old (my Jesus year), with a seven-year-old, five-year-old twins, and a three-year-old. My husband, a teacher, now had to instruct over one hundred of his students from home in our small apartment in New York, which had become a classroom for our four small children and an executive space for me. Talk about chaos! I had been a clinical assistant professor, and in my role for the past four years, I felt like an expert. I had been getting promoted, recognized, and celebrated. I took on a new role (I had negotiated a significantly higher salary) in a new city, not knowing that the world was about to completely shut down. We purchased our first home in the middle of a pandemic. We had a huge back yard, each kid had their own room, and there was a huge basement that doubled as a gym and my husband's man cave. I even built a shed that turned out to be one of my favorite sanctuaries! The entire world had shut down. I recognize the privilege of my home and outdoor space juxtaposed with the death and disarray caused by the pandemic. I am not minimizing the toll of the pandemic, but for me personally, at the outset of the pandemic, life was good.

I started in this role and was immediately thrown into this work from my home environment. With little to no guidance, I began to adapt and figure it out. I was overseeing multimillion dollar statewide programs, leading quality improvement and education and being the voice for nurses, who were seen as heroes throughout this pandemic. I was overseeing programs on wellness and workforce while my own wellness was slowly deteriorating. Something had to be wrong with me, right? I had a dream job, dream house, made amazing new friends, and my family was thriving. I realized that the work environment I had entered was not only toxic but not supportive of me.

I was a young accomplished smart woman of color doing amazing things and having a huge impact, but I was met with micro-aggressive behaviors and facing a "pet to threat" phenomenon. I was sought after, desired, and recruited because I was young, Black, and talented but soon realized that was a threat to an organization that had no intention of changing the status quo. We were in the middle of such a critical time. With the death of George Floyd, police brutality and racial injustices had become priorities of many organizations; however, many remained silent. Everything was colliding all at once. So now what? I moved out here and gave up so much in the process, but what did I gain?

Fast forward and it's February 2022. We have been in this pandemic for two years. Countless lives have been lost. People are struggling with mental health, and the uncertainty of what comes next is heavy. I quit my job (BIG SMILE). I am so thrilled to have made a decision that has brought me peace while solidifying for me life expectations on what I will and will not tolerate. I started my own consulting business, and opportunities have been flowing as if the floodgates were opened! I am intentional and present with the time I spend with my family. I make my own rules, and I get to finally finish this little project I started a few years ago called my PhD. So, while I may not know exactly what comes next, I have learned to prioritize what matters most. As I close this essay, I am about to meet with a summer camp director in Hawaii looking for a nurse, so my family and I might be soaking in the sun and pro surfing this summer 2022! But whatever comes next. I am more ready than I have ever been to take it on with excellence.

Sandy Cayo DNP, FNP-BC
Mother of Jeremiah (seven), Theresa (five), Josephine (five),
and Jasmine (three)*
Healthcare Change Agent
* ages at the onset of the pandemic

An Escape to Iceland, a Cross-Country Epic, and Other Misadventures in Pandemic Parenting

No one is ever quite ready; everyone is always caught off guard. Parenthood chooses you. And you open your eyes, look at what you've got, say "Oh, my gosh," and recognize that of all the balls there ever were, this is the one you should not drop. It's not a question of choice.

—Marisa de los Santos

My husband jokingly calls me an "optimistic pessimist"; I'm apt to anticipate the worst-case scenario but plan for it, as best I can, with a good sense of humour and bucket loads of research. Unsurprisingly, my approach to parenting and working through the pandemic has been through this lens. Over the last two years, I have found myself repeatedly planning for specific outcomes, experiencing very different and unexpected outcomes, and learning how to be at peace with my scrambled best laid plans.

In fall of 2019, I was flirting with a career change. Although I loved the research work I did with museums, I wondered if I should return to school and study medicine. For the first time in years, I felt like I could explore new directions as both of my children would finally be in school. Obviously, the spring of 2020 did not go as anyone planned, and I ended up with an anatomy class, a psychology class, several live consulting projects, and two children home full time in lockdown. In the early days of the pandemic, every hour felt like a mountain. It was an endless marathon of getting my six-year-old settled on Zoom, entertaining my toddler, working, attending virtual classes, supporting my overwhelmed husband (a health center administrator), and still somehow finding the time to bake a few loaves of sourdough (because didn't we all?).

My brother and his fiancé had been visiting when the lockdown went into effect, and as remote workers, they decided to stay "until this blows over." They stayed for five months. We bubbled with my extended family and found incredible joy in frequent family dinners, epic water balloon fights (kids and adults), board games, movie nights, and gardening. My older child thrived in remote schooling, whereas my younger child, though sweet and joyful most of the time, struggled more with our divided attention. We got through those first six months with a few new worry lines and an overwhelming appreciation for the gift of time together. We played hard, and we worried hard.

The museums that had supported my audience research firm for years were all shuttered. The education programs I evaluated were in a state of chaos, as they tried to transform in-person education into remote learning. My plans for exploring a career shift dried up, as I took over the role of primary parent while my husband worked insanely long hours trying to keep the community health center running. We watched the news, checked our phones for COVID-19 updates, and spoke in hushed voices to try to keep the little ears in our household from picking up on our worry. As fall of 2020 approached, my husband and I confronted the reality of more remote school and a nowhere near normal childhood for our children. So, what did we do? Naturally, we decided to move to Iceland for a few months for a last gasp of pre-COVID-19 life.

Iceland was a miracle for exactly four weeks. We had a sweet apartment by the sea, the kids swam in the local pool almost every day, we saw family, we went to bakeries, and my children started school (sans masks). There was no spread of COVID-19 in Iceland at that time. And then, with humbling speed, COVID-19 ripped through the country like wildfire, and I was quarantined from an exposure to a positive colleague. I had met with him in his office, door shut, and not a mask to speak of. There was a need, he assured me, for audience research work in Iceland. I could remake myself as an expat and give my career new wings in this alien landscape. I was so wonderfully hopeful after that meeting; I picked the kids up from school, and we went to the pool for a soak. Later that night, I got the stomach sinking email that my colleague tested positive for COVID-19 after our meeting. I was put into eight days of government-mandated quarantine in my grandmother-in-law's tiny summer house overlooking a beautiful lake. Miraculously, I did not end up testing positive, but quarantining away from my children was heartbreaking, and I promised myself I would never take a sloppy kiss or sleepy cuddle for granted again.

When my quarantine ended, and I reunited my sweet children (and very tired husband), we started talking about our next move. Iceland was experiencing high COVID-19 rates, and remote work in a distant time zone had become unsustainable for my husband. We decided it was time to go. Cases in the US that fall were rising fast, and the air travel it would take to get back to California was looking like an excellent way to catch COVID-19. So naturally, we decided a better approach to COVID-19 risk management would be to buy a camper and a car that could tow it on the East Coast and drive all the way across the US with two young children.

Over the next few weeks, we returned to the US, learned how to hitch and tow a camper, charted a course through fourteen states, and had remarkable adventures. We marveled at the fall colors in Pennsylvania, hiked with bison in Kansas, slid down the Great Sand Dunes in Colorado, and took in the glory of Arches National Park in Utah. We truly lived in the moment with our bold (and potentially stupid) choice to buy our camper, made magical memories as a family, and gave our kids the adventure of a lifetime while the pandemic raged around us. Since our epic Icelandic and cross-country adventures, we have stayed closer to home and navigated a return to in-person school for both boys, a new job as a communications director for me, and a continually stressful but rewarding job in healthcare for my husband.

As we enter 2022, I am definitely not where I thought I would be, and I am at peace with that. The pandemic has taught me that my best laid plans and deep research dives will not always pan out in the way I anticipate. Instead of sweating new twists, I'm striving to appreciate each moment and be mindfully open to new opportunities as they arise. The pandemic has made me more aware than ever that I never want to let my children down and that I would go (and have gone) to the edges of the world to give them a chance to live fully. My hope for my children is that they continue to live boldly with the confidence of knowing that grand adventures are attainable and that, even in the face of trying times, there is beauty and fun to be found in the world if you work to create it.

Ashlan Falletta-Cowden, MA
Mother of Stefan Bjorn (SB) (six) and Anders (two)*
Audience Research Consultant and Director of Communications
*ages at the onset of the pandemic

COVID-19 through the Eyes of a Single, Working Mom

Courage is not having the strength to go on;
it's going on when you don't have the strength.

—*Theodore Roosevelt*

In March 2020, I was working at a YMCA in Southington, Connecticut, as the health and wellness supervisor. I was so proud when I got that promotion, from working as a personal trainer to now being a supervisor. I was proud to show my kids that hard work pays off. What we knew of COVID-19 then was limited, so it seemed so abstract and hard to believe until gyms shut down, until everything shut down. It was scary. I had never been released from any job I'd ever had, nor had I ever collected or been dependent on the state to pay my bills. I was always proud of what I could provide for my children, so that was a blow to my ego.

Being furloughed from the YMCA from March until June had its benefits but also its difficulties. I vowed I would take this time to be completely present with my children because I knew I would rarely have this uninterrupted time home with them. The difficult part was being forced to collect unemployment while being a completely able-bodied person very capable of making my own living. That was hard for me to accept. I decided to start my own limited liability company (LLC) so I would have a backup plan in case I permanently lost my job at the YMCA. This way I could see clients virtually during lockdown and then in person whenever it was safe again to do so. An added challenge was supervising three children during virtual homeschool. They were in three different grades and dealt with this challenge in three completely different ways. My oldest was thankfully self-sufficient and only needed limited guidance. My middle son struggled tremendously—not only with the focus and attention span required to learn online but also with the technology. He also lacked the complete desire to do any of the required assignments. My youngest was in preschool and had little to no work to do, so keeping her occupied while being available to help her brothers was a challenge. Any kind of virtual work I had to do for my business further took my attention away from them, and it was all a difficult balancing act. All of this coupled with having to tell my three social children that they couldn't see and play with friends was heartbreaking.

We were allowed to return to work at the YMCA in June 2020. I decided to run my business concurrently and maintain my financial back-up plan. I remained at the YMCA from June until August, when I was officially permanently laid off. That was an emotional day to say the least. My business was not yet making enough money, and I had no idea how I would support my kids, let alone pay bills and keep a roof over our heads. I knew I could collect unemployment, but there was no way to know if it would be enough to support a mortgage. At the time, I had been trying to refinance my house into my name only. With the loss of my job, that process came to a complete halt. I was devastated. I had always wanted to prove that I could support a house and everything for my kids on my own, and now I definitely could not.

Nevertheless, I had to keep going and find a way to make my business work. With the kids back in school in the fall, I dedicated everything to growing my business. Although in-person school felt risky, I knew it was where my kids needed to be. I felt all of them, especially my middle son, would suffer academically if they continued school virtually, and I needed to be able to work on increasing my income—something that would be extremely difficult with all three children trying to learn online. Slowly but surely my business grew, mostly by word of mouth. I was extremely lucky to have long-time clients stay with me during the transition and move with me to my home gym. I also felt lucky to have the work at home option, as there were still times when COVID-19 forced people to stay home, and I was able to train them virtually. I was also able to help the kids with school, if need be, when they would have the occasional virtual school day. I was able to remove myself from state assistance, and I now have more than thirty-five clients and have been running my business from home for a year and a half.

This experience has taught me so many things. The ability to be completely present with my children was invaluable to me. Although lockdown brought so many fears and challenges, I treasure that time I had with them, to be with them and enjoy them. While losing my job was extremely scary, it forced me to do something for myself that I might not have otherwise—to venture out on my own and start my own business. It allowed me to be my own boss and to have the flexibility to work around my kids schedule and be there for them when they needed me while still working full time. I can honestly say this experience has changed me for the better. I have so much pride in my business and what it has become. I can show my kids that if you work hard, you can turn no matter what life throws at you into something positive. I love that I can be there for my clients and also for my kids. My kids can also see both me and my clients working hard at taking care of their minds and their bodies and how important that is not only in these challenging times but going forward as well.

Lisa Fields
Mother of Ian (nine), Samuel (seven), and Tessa (four)*
Certified Personal Trainer and Nutrition Coach
Certified Life Coach
*ages at the onset of the pandemic

Pandemic Enlightenment

Until you lean into your heart,
you cannot witness the divine light within.

—Ziba Ansari-Orlando

M y daughter was two and a half years old when the pandemic started in the US. At work, I recall the long hours working as a hospital pharmacist in what were the beginning days of the pandemic. I could sense the fear everywhere surrounding the many unanswered questions about COVID-19. I felt exhausted from watching patients succumb to the virus and the difficulty of witnessing the "no visitor" rule that was designated to protect and prevent the spread of the disease.

At home, it was a different story. Everything was quiet, serene, and spiritual in every sense. My environment enabled me to garden alongside my husband and our daughter—spending every free moment in the yard, picking weeds, clearing space, planting, as well as creating and communing with Mother Nature. We were one with the trees, the sky, the hills, and of course all the animals near and far: the deer, turkey, squirrels, opossum, chickens and even a few California King snakes. As the days went on, my connection to the source grew stronger. At nights when I was putting my daughter to sleep, I received many downloads. I would hear random thoughts that would then merge into ideas. In the coming months, I began to extrapolate and put together what my soul was telling me was my mission in this lifetime.

Given the pandemic stressors at work, I thoughtfully designed a life at home that reflected the world I wanted to live in: peaceful and connected to the source. It was through this connection that my greatest insight emerged—the realization that I want to work with parents and help children be the best versions of themselves. This awakening led me to write a book for parents and children.

My daughter was the source of inspiration, and she was my connection to source and higher dimensions. My daughter also provided the link to my ancestral lineage; she allowed me to connect to my Persian heritage and its long historical foundation rooted in poets and mystics, such as Rumi and Hafez. It was a deeper than realized source of light and love. Along with my own interest and passion for deep spiritual work, I spent numerous hours on Zoom classes with various teachers, masters, and healers during my free moments, and might I mention there was a myriad of free and amazing offerings during the pandemic. Everyone from around the world was pulling together to help, pray, and uplift humanity and consciousness. This pilgrimage into my soul deepened with each day. I remember when I had the idea to write and self-publish my book *The ABCs of Life to Nourish the Mind and Soul of Children*. There was no ego, no fear, and no small sense of self that got in my way. It was a calling, and I was determined to find a way to make it happen. It was my heart talking to me louder than it had my entire life.

I was ready to start strengthening my clairsentience, and each day, I practiced listening to my inner voice. My journey involved energy work, yoga, meditation, visual imagery, and the ultimate source of all—connecting to the energy of my daughter. She has been able to help me formulate my life's purpose, and I continue to do whatever I can to assist my daughter to develop her dreams, her desires, and help her blossom into who she is meant to be. I am grateful the pandemic provided the impetus for me to move in the direction of my calling. As I continue to work as a hospital pharmacist, I've been making steps toward my calling by starting a website, enrolling in a year-long parent coaching program, and providing Energy Medicine Yoga (EMYoga) to help other human beings strengthen their connection to energy and intuition. My ultimate goal is to serve as a heartful parent coach, empowering other parents on a similar journey.

Ziba Ansari-Orlando
Mother of Isabella Arianna Orlando (two)*
Hospital Pharmacist
Energy Medicine Yoga (EMYoga) Instructor, 200 YTT Hatha Yoga

Certified Parent Coach
Business owner: A Heartful Path
*age at the onset of the pandemic

Riptides of Self

Carry on, brave mother who tries when she's tired.
Carry on, brave mother who gives unconditionally.
Carry on, Brave mother who cries because she loves.
Carry on, brave mother who hopes without answers.
Carry on, Brave mother who loves without expectations.
Carry on, Brave mother. Carry on.
—Rachel Marie Martin, The Brave Art of Motherhood 75

I don't think there has ever been a period in my life when I felt flooded by every facet of my identity all at once—mother, wife, daughter, sister, friend, academic, mental health professional, public scholar, and Greek Orthodox Christian woman—than since the onset of this global pandemic. It was as if overnight every one of my roles and responsibilities kicked into high gear, each competing for my care, attention, and responsiveness. In reflection, it was during this period that I realized exactly who I am and exactly who the world needs me to be—every one of these persons, all at once.

The integrated parts of my collective whole have always intrigued me. I knew them to be intricate from the time of my childhood. So many facets. So many inlets. So many tides. Some made sense. Others did not. Then motherhood.

What is it like for the world to have to share your mother? This is a gift and a guilt that has vexed me from pregnancy. I knew too well that I would not cease being all these things after my children were born, and I also knew that I would never compromise their upbringing. Thus, this catch-22 unfolded well before my now seven-year-old twin girls were born. It is something that I had to accept about myself from the beginning—my children would have to share their mother with the community and perhaps even the larger world. This was a treaty I had to negotiate with myself, as it defied everything conventional that my traditional Greek upbringing posits about mothering.

My girls were in kindergarten in March 2020 when they packed "two weeks" worth of their schoolwork for this short pause in their education—a pause that would roll into the remainder of that school year and most of the next. The home front became the "all" front—home, office, school, gym, and even church. I worked full time, started a mental health blog on matters related to coping with the pandemic, was interviewed by several national podcasts/videocasts, spoke at different parent and professional women workshops, and administered our church's school program. My girls had to witness all of the above; many times, they had to wait for their turn or merely settle for sitting in the same room as their mother and working by her side in order to feel her comfort. I oversaw my children's schoolwork with much leniency and mercy. The same holds true about their behavior. I cared more about their psychological safety and mental health than anything else.

Some days, I felt like I was on top of my game. Other days, I felt like I could crumble. I had to strike down my anxiety 90 percent of my waking day, only to be too exhausted to deal with it in the remaining 10 percent after all responsibilities for that day were completed or shelved. So, Netflix romcoms won. Every. Single. Time.

It is extremely hard to reduce my lessons learned as a working mother during the time of a global pandemic into one insight or key takeaway. I can best compare it to driving a five-speed car on a curvy, relentless racetrack; I switched into any mode that called upon me, all in a moment's notice. My biggest revelation was this: As a working mother, the rules didn't apply to me. I don't think they ever will. It is about rising in the moment, reflecting in the quiet, and knowing that I embody great love—for my family, for my career, and for the larger world.

Evelyn Bilias Lolis, PhD
*Mother to Thalia (six) and Natasha (six)**
Educational Psychologist, Research Scientist, Blogger
*ages at the onset of the pandemic

Discussion

The premise of this very book rests on how to re-imagine and rebuild after such physical and emotional unrest. In psychology, agency is the term for the perception of personal control that one has over their actions and related consequences of those actions (Bandura). It rests in the human capacity to direct one's life and regulate accordingly (Bandura). One's sense of agency is the belief that they are an agent and play an active role in how their life unfolds (Frie). According to researchers, agency is a multidimensional entity that depends on biological, affective (feelings/emotions), and sociocultural factors that govern one's circumstance and their interpretation of it (Frie).

Psychological agency is linked with the pursuit of meaning and purpose and can be used as fuel for reimagination and rebirth (Frie). It involves one's capacity to flexibly reconstruct and architect one's experience in a manner that provides meaning, reward, and personal fulfillment. The pandemic period certainly had its share of restrictions that readily led to feelings of suffocation. Additionally, the ongoing and evolving nature of COVID-19, with its variants and spurts, led to what popular psychology coined "pandemic flux syndrome," or feelings of dysphoria that emerged from the vicious cycle of anxiety, unrest, and hopelessness to temporary hope, normalcy, and illusions of peace that were in perpetual flux (Cuddy and Riley). How do you create meaning and agency out of flux and instability?

This task was accomplished in a multitude of ways based on the narratives provided in this chapter. For some, this involved an emergence of an entirely new pursuit while others used quiet inspiration, nature, and travel to shape the course of their family experience. Emily, a widowed mother, faculty developer, and sole caretaker for her tween/ teen youngsters discovered that agency became "baked" into the activities that held the family together during the most trying times. It did not unfold in a grand calculated plan but in the subtle day to day rituals that brought meaning, connection, and resilience into the home. As Emily said, "My greatest insight from mothering and working during the pandemic is that my children's world is the world I create for them."

For the mothers in this chapter, agency meant taking action by rolling up their sleeves and enacting the grit required to activate what was best for their family and reclaim autonomy (Cuddy and Pearce). In several cases, this meant re-imagining their professional career, reshaping existing work structures, or even thinking creatively about ways to spend the pandemic displacement. As a divorced single mother, Lisa's narrative describes her struggle with a work furlough that led to unemployment and how in the space in between these two transitions, the building of a new virtual nutrition/fitness business emerged. This small enterprise ultimately grew into a sustainable home gym fitness coaching facility. Agency fuelled her drive to move from unemployment to independence, which led to the development of her own business in order to best support herself and her three children. In the midst of her job loss and a global pandemic, she refashioned her life into one that re-imagined her professional skillset, work-life balance, and familial priorities.

Ziba, a mother with a hospital pharmaceutical career and a toddler at home, found herself moved by her inner voice and quality time spent in nature and in connection with her family. It was during this time that she discovered her calling to offer a broader mark on the world and write a book that would help parents raise healthy children. She described her agency using the following narrative: "I began to extrapolate and put together what my soul was telling me was my mission in this lifetime.... It was my heart talking to me louder than it had my entire life." Ziba knew that it was not a matter of if but how this calling (her book) was going to come into fruition: "I was determined to find a way to make it happen."

Similarly, Evelyn, an educational psychologist and academic, affirmed that her calling involved nurturing an anxious world through interviews, podcasts, and writings while nurturing a stable home environment. She described her children as growing accustomed to sharing their mother with the world. Perhaps this speaks to a different layer of agency—the global agency shared by mothers who work outside of the home and raise children.

One can argue that agency is unabating in the life of a mother who is accountable to work outside the home while also being accountable to her family. This level of multitasking and constant role shifting invites flexibility, creative problem solving, and agility in managing moving targets. As Evelyn described, "For working mothers, the rules never apply." The onset of the lockdown might have displaced the physical demands of their roles, but in no way did it displace their complexity or their shifting nature.

Agency transformed the ever-complex equation of mothering and careering to now include a 2.0 pandemic version. Thus, psychological agency also includes a deep sense of knowing what you need and being agile in your resourcefulness (Bandura). For Ashlan, a mother of two with a career in marketing and research, this time of uncertainty and quarantine afforded the option to travel as a pandemic calling. Her journey led her first to traveling to Iceland during the COVID-19 outbreak and then to purchasing a camper to travel the US with her family when the COVID-19 rates were low, and Iceland's were peaking. Ashlan's awakening was that despite life's plot twists, agency could be redirected through open mindedness, creativity, and resources. Likewise, Anastasia, an English literature PhD candidate, a mother of two school-aged children, and wife to an emergency room director and physician found agency through identifying with strong maternal literary figures: "They inspired and invigorated me. Here were two women, albeit fictional, passing through some version of personal hell, creating environments of nurture and safety for their sons, and, through their trials, arriving at capable and blooming versions of themselves." This mother found resolve in the literary maternal heroines and in moments of quiet family reflection. Anastasia further said: "As soul sustaining and as important as the work was and continues to be, both personally and professionally, in the pandemic environment of uncertainty and fear, I chose some form of self-preservation."

Finally, Sandy, a healthcare change agent and mother to three elementary school children began a new role and was called to oversee multimillion dollar statewide programs leading quality improvement for frontline nurses, only to realize that her own wellness was worsening. Her agency—nestled in reflection, prayer, and self-inventory—allowed her to make the change and quit her job, which was needed for her personal and familial wellbeing. For all women whose narratives are depicted in this chapter, their experiences were elected choices that created a reality for family life that offered a unique freedom at a time of heightened constraint.

Steps to Re-imagining

Psychologist Albert Bandura defined agency as containing four key elements: intentionality, forethought, self-regulation, and self-reflection. The collection of narratives presented in this chapter speak to these very entities—a mindful knowing of where one is and where one needs to be, the forethought and grit to endure the stake at hand, the composure to stay in the role and shift into any other role as needed, and the reflection to now sit back and write a narrative for of the experience. Here we are. Full circle.

Agency is a powerful, self-affirming tool when one is able to recognize it in themselves. In the perpetual multitasking loop that is motherhood and careering, agency can go readily undetected in the grind of the day to day. Agency, however, deserves to be recognized and celebrated. At the heart of agency lies resilience and the mustering of strength to prevail, persist, and rise. Creating routine opportunities to recognize and celebrate the agency we demonstrate as mothers in the big and small pockets of our lives is one small adjustment worth re-imagining.

Reflective Prompts

1. Agency is not an all or nothing concept. We can show more agency in some aspects of our lives and less in others. Reflect on your pandemic experience. What examples of psychological agency did you employ with respect to your career?

2. Again, take a moment to reflect on your pandemic experience. What examples of psychological agency did you employ this time with respect to mothering and home life?

3. Identify two to three individuals in your personal or professional life who empower your sense of agency or your ability to feel like you can take charge and conquer goals and challenges. Send them a note or call them and let them know that they serve this purpose for you. Express your gratitude for their presence in your life. Knowing that they empower agency in you and that you are grateful for this role will reinforce their ability to continue to do so due to the increased awareness you have provided them.

4. How can you promote feelings of agency in your children? List two to three ways you help your children feel empowered to act

in a way that will help them attain a greater sense of esteem, self, or competence. Write down these specific actions and share them with your child (if age appropriate). Lastly, make a plan for practicing and celebrating agency in your home life.

5. What aspects of the "world you created" during the pandemic would you like to keep into play as you go forward in re-imagining mothering and careering today? Write them down and keep them somewhere visible to serve as a reminder and anchor.

Works Cited

Bandura, Albert. "The Reconstrual of 'Free Will' from the Agentic Perspective of Social Cognitive Theory." *Are We Free? Psychology and Free Will*, edited by John Baer, James Kaufman, and Roy Baumeister, Oxford University Press, 2008, pp. 86-127.

Bandura, Albert. "Toward a Psychology of Human Agency: Pathways and Reflections." *Perspectives on Psychological Science*, vol. 13, no. 2, 2018, pp. 130-36.

Cuddy, Amy and Jill Ellyn Riley. "Why This Stage of the Pandemic Makes Us So Anxious." *Washington Post,* 11 Aug. 2021, https://www.washingtonpost.com/outlook/2021/08/11/pandemic-anxiety-psychology-delta/. Accessed 6 June 2023.

Cuddy, Amy, and Nicholas Pearce. "One Reason so Many Are Quitting: We Want Control Over Our Lives Again." *Washington Post*, 16 Dec. 2021, https://www.washingtonpost.com/outlook/2021/12/16/great-resignation-power-regret-psychology/. Accessed 6 June 2023.

De Los Santos, Maria. *Love Walked In.* Plume Press, 2006.

Frie, Roger. *Psychological Agency: Theory, Practice, and Culture.* MIT Press, 2008.

Gorman, Amanda. *Call Us What We Carry.* Viking Books, 2021.

Holy Bible. King James Version. Christian Art Publishers, 2016.

Martin, Rachel Marie. *The Brave Art of Motherhood: Fight Fear, Gain Confidence, and Find Yourself Again.* Waterbrook Press, 2018.

Rowling, J.K. "Single motherhood is the Thing I am Most Proud Of." *Huffington Post*, 18 Sept. 2013, https://www.huffpost.com/entry/jk-rowling-single-motherh_n_3950648

Conclusion

Central Awakenings

The narratives in this book share commonality in the broad themes of self-compassion, mindfulness, gratitude, mothering in community, growing stronger, and agency—creeds for the manifesto on moving forward. So here we are, arriving at the crossroad of re-imagining mothering and careering women with a collective wisdom available to us.

A central depiction throughout all our stories is that we were all attempting to find our way, or on most days simply trying to stay afloat. Our narratives vividly capture that we did so while caring for our families and children of all ages (with some even giving birth during the pandemic) while additionally maintaining careers. The image of Atlas holding up the world is perhaps the most apropos of wage-earning mothers during the pandemic. We were shouldering it all. Yet we made our way through this pivotal and challenging time, gaining rich insights that manifested through the tears, worry, and many pervasive unknowns. These learnings are worthy of being uplifted, spoken about often, and fundamentally used to restructure the expectations of wage-earning mothers. We need to protect these findings, so they are not lost. We need not return to life as it were pre-pandemic. We must, in fact, not go back but rather use these voices to propel forward.

The voices for self-compassion remind us of our humanness and the need to show mercy toward ourselves and the demands society places on us—demands that are at times unhealthy and unyielding. Self-compassion in mothering and careering involves actively challenging the guilt that drains our energy; it is a guilt ignited by perfectionism and the expectation to biconically and magically meet the needs of everyone and everything around us. Mercy toward oneself needs to be reclaimed as a sign of strength, wisdom, and groundedness. Increased self-compassion and an awakened sense of self are what led many women to demand more equitable, flexible, and healthy work expectations post-pandemic (Corbett). The great resignation eventually evolved into what economists and organizational psychologists call "the great renegotiation," with women and other wage-earning members of the workforce advocating for healthier work cultures and more competitive benefits and pay (Women In Revenue). Self-compassion is the impetus for this reclaiming.

The voices for mindfulness prompt us to pause in the moment and truly be alive in the messy, the difficult, and the blissful. The world may (hopefully) never stop again in the same way; hence, we have to create and preserve the "stops"—the natural pauses that enact the senses and allow us to be awake and present in our work, home, and relationships. Mindful awareness and groundedness in mothering and careering are choices that we need to commit to and to practice, in order for them to become a way of life.

Likewise, the voices for gratitude demonstrate the need for mothers to scan their environments for the good and stop to savor it. A type of mindfulness, gratitude embodies an active will to nestle oneself in the gifts that each day brings amid chaos and uncertainty; it expresses appreciation for the moments and individuals that fill us. Through such recognitions, we keep at the forefront pieces of resilience found in our corner that we can lean into and draw strength from.

The voices for connectedness and community remind us that although mothering can feel highly isolative, we are not alone in our plight. There is tremendous strength to be found in a community of others around us who support us, lift us up, and at times even carry us if we let them. Connectedness is a wellspring and lifeforce—a tie that binds us as mothers, as women, and as human beings.

The voices for grit speak to the tenacity that lies within us. Grit is the ability to muster the courage and strength to make it to the other side of challenges, obstacles, and even crises. There is tremendous grit involved in mothering, and perhaps even more so for those who elect to maintain careers while raising a family being accountable to expectations of home and work life. Grit is the lubricant for getting through challenging situations physically and emotionally stronger.

Lastly, the voices for agency champion the human spirit and the resolve present in each one of us if we recognize it. It is the "maternal surge" that evolves effervescently and directs the ship of our lives as we captain the duties of the home and the workplace. Agency is the part of us that digs into the difficult and steers challenges and/or goals to their resting point. For most mothers, agency is on autopilot, secretly navigating the tides of life. The minute we decide to invite it into our conscious awareness we discover yet another redefined self that is waiting eagerly to journey with us.

Final Thoughts on Motherhood Re-imagined

We all entered and exited the pandemic in various physical and emotional states, with our own lived experiences, our wage-earning work demands, and our unique family structures, needs, and priorities. As the essays in this collection have elucidated, we do not claim there is only one insight rather that there is diversity in the meaning assigned to our struggles and experiences, which led to these awakenings.

The story of mothers who both maintained careers and mothered is one that needs to be heard. As evident in each of these narratives, COVID-19 changed our lives by pulling out from under us our support networks, our routines, and perceptions of safety and stability. We were fundamentally changed from mothering and working through the pandemic. We were stretched thin by home and work demands. This relentless push and pull is the reason we sought to solicit these narratives and write this book. Our worlds have shifted and in tandem so have we. Our hope in writing was that the cosmic shifts that redefined us and made us slow down, appreciate more, shed what was no longer working, relearn who we are and how we define ourselves, be intentional, and seek out better work life balances do not simply disappear. Our intent was to highlight that through it all, we have changed.

As Anna, a mother of a preschooler and one-year old twins and a nurse practitioner supervisor, offers, "Can we demand a work-life balance that works? You bet we can.... The system must change because we have changed." We recognize the unsustainability of societal expectations on wage-earning mothers who juggle a career and the raising of a family not only during the pandemic but pre-COVID-19 as well. The pressures placed on mothers were not realistic, yet we survived a time where social structures were painstakingly closed, causing us to find a new way. These collective insights must be not only archived but used to re-imagine the life of working mothers everywhere. For all mothers who found themselves navigating uncharted waters: We hear you. We see you. We wrote this for you. We each have a story that deserves to be told and a life to be re-imagined and lived. These depictions are not meant to simply uplift women and both their paid and unpaid work but rather to shine a light on the people we have become because of what we have individually and collectively experienced: transformation.

Our journey was not the same nor was it equitable. If we are to embrace our humanness, we must understand that the impact of the pandemic varied. Some experienced the pandemic easier, whereas others had far worse experiences. In this way, the pandemic was not a one-size-fits-all journey. Yes, we all experienced and lived through a global crisis. Yes, in this case, "we were all in the same storm" (i.e., COVID-19) yet "not in the same boat" (Friedman and Satterthwaite 53). This analogy is the anchor by which we frame the findings and conclusion of this book. Our boats differed home to home, person to person, mother to mother. Our financial resources, familial and marital stressors, personality traits and tendencies, health histories, and mental health predispositions all affected how we perceived, experienced, and coped with the pandemic. In this way, some of us were clinging to a piece of driftwood, whereas others had yachts and every imaginable floating device and vessel in between.

Similarly, how we grow and heal from this lived experience differs from one person to the next, one family to the next. These thirty-three women have written and shared their truths in hopes to inspire, to make sense of the experience, and to show and allow others how to begin to reflect on their personal journeys. Ingenuity, creativity, and tenacity became the beacons by which to survive these days as a wage-earning mother. The learnings from these women of mindfulness, gratitude, self-compassion, community, grit, and agency are freely available to us; they simply require practice and conscious awareness. All we have to do is choose to lean into the work required to integrate them into our lives. We hope that through the reflective prompts offered at the end of each chapter, you can think about your experience and can boldly share your story, tell story, and write your own essay that defines how you have re-imagined motherhood and career. This is how we rebuild and emerge anew.

We are custodians of this moment in time—a time when mothers working in both careers and the unpaid sectors of their homes are emerging from a global pandemic. Each personal account is worth preserving and telling. As a caterpillar forms a chrysalis and emerges a butterfly, so too did women in career enter the pandemic and emerge anew with insights to improve their working life and to recenter and re-imagine mothering and career. The tenuous part of not going back to simply the way things were for wage-earning mothers working post-pandemic is why the image of the butterfly is so crucial. The fleeting nature of the pandemic's insights has resulted in the world wanting to move on again at a pace that was, and will continue to be, unsustainable for mothers with careers. We learned from the pandemic, whether we wanted to or not. The pandemic brought insights to us about our work and our mothering that begged us to redefine and re-imagine our lives. It took something this severe to unite women to say this is not sustainable, and we must use this collective force to catapult us forward for a better, more sustainable, more reimaged working mother future. "Rather than rebuilding what we once knew, let us be the architects of a new world" (Fulweiler 1).

We are different, the world is different, and honoring who we are and how we have grown is imperative for the self-development of wage-earning mothers everywhere. We must strive beyond simply making the focus of each day to keep our head above water. Rather, we must move to demand and create a culture of structures, systems, and supports that yield the bridges vital to achieving greatness in our personal family lives and in our professional worlds.

Empowerment is found in the authority, strength, and renewed confidence that arose during a time of shared experience. Our personal agency lies in the recognition that within us resides a compelling story for which we hold the pen and editing rights. Our collective empowerment lies in the force that weds our narratives across careers and cultures —as mothers—a societal force, a global force, a life force. The insights we choose to safely harbor from the trying moments of life are the gold lines to our restoration, which serendipitously connect our severed pieces together like the art of Kintsugi. We encourage you to continue to explore your re-imagined self, shine your light, assert your truths, and embrace your worth as a mother who serves both home and career.

Works Cited

Corbett, Holly. "How Companies Can Reverse the Great Resignation by Supporting Working Mothers. *Forbes*, 21 Apr. 2022, https://www. forbes.com/sites/hollycorbett/2022/04/21/how-companies-can-reverse-the-great-resignation-by-supporting-working-mothers/?sh=4978e561314f. Accessed 7 June 2023.

Friedman, May, and Emily Satterthwaite. "Same Storm, Different Boats: Some Thoughts on Gender, Race, and Class in the Time of COVID-19." *Mothers, Mothering, and COVID-19: Dispatches from the Pandemic*, edited by Andrea O'Reilly and Fiona Joy Green, Demeter Press, 2021, pp. 53-64.

Fulweiler Robinson W., et al. "Rebuild the Academy: Supporting Academic Mothers during COVID-19 and Beyond." *PLoS Biology*, vol. 19, no. 3, 2021, pp. 1-11.

Women in Revenue. "The Great Renegotiation: The Definitive 2022 State of Women in Revenue Report." *Squarespace*, March 2022, https://static1.squarespace.com/static/5d1536430653fc00012a 48f7/t/6245f85654aefd2c8b035a98/1648752727570/WIR_eBook_ Definitive_2022_Report_Final-3-29.pdf?utm_campaign=WIR+e-Book. Accessed 7 June 2023.

It is endemic now.

It is endemic now,
But we are not the same,
We are not who we were before COVID came.

The pandemic exposed the cracks,
The fault lines and fractures,
Flaws in the very fabric we'd built our lives around.

We tripped over the chasm in the ground
And hastily built the bridge
That would buoy us.

The pandemic pulled the sails from our ships,
Pushed us in a new direction,
One that has brought us here.

Yet we unearthed beauty from this new direction
Unveiled hidden truths
And awakened to the challenge.

The stories are ours to own
Inside our homes and out.

We are here... standing strong
In an altered world,
Ourselves, our lives re-imagined.
We are here to be heard.
We are here to be honored.

Resources

We invite you to a social media platform, specifically a group we have created, to ensure all those wishing to share their insights and experiences have a safe community in which to do so. We encourage you to join and be a part of this conversation, using our Facebook Group titled "Re-imagining Mothering and Career: Insights from a time of Crisis": https://www.facebook.com/groups/400341808797568/.

Furthermore, we have compiled the following list of resources for continued exploration of re-imagining motherhood and career:

Wellbeing, Self-Compassion, and Burnout Prevention Resources

- drbilias.com: https://www.drbilias.com
- Greater Good Science Center: https://greatergood.berkeley.edu
- Positive Psychology Blog: https://positivepsychology.com/blog
- Self-Compassion Resources from Dr. Kristen Neff: https://self-compassion.org
- Thrive Global Blog (Burnout Prevention Platform) https://thriveglobal.com/stories

Mindfulness Resources and Apps

- Calm: https://www.calm.com
- Headspace: https://headspace.com
- Mindful Mamas: https://mindfulmamasclub.com
- Smiling Mind (free app): https://www.smilingmind.com.au

Gratitude Resources and Apps

- Gratitude Happiness Journal: https://apps.apple.com/us/app/gratitude-happiness-journal/id1372575227
- Presently: https://presently-app.firebaseapp.com

Suggested Reading

- Casares, Whitney. *The Working Mom Blueprint.* The American Academy of Pediatrics, 2021.
- Saujani, Reshma. *Pay Up The Future of Women and Work (and Why it's Different Than You Think).* One Signal Publishers/Atria, 2022.

Special Thanks

To Karoline Morton, an undergraduate BSN Fairfield University Egan School of Nursing and Health Studies student, for assisting the authors during their initial literature review.

Dedications
with Love

To my MILE—Maggie, Isabel, Leo, and Ethan—may you develop grit to follow your aspirations and take the paths that bring you joy. Yet I hope the compass will always bring you together as the fabric of our crazy chaos as a family of six is and forever will be part of your narrative. I know that as you grow and the house quiets, I will miss this time with my entire heart. Maggie you are the kindest, most compassionate soul, caring deeply for everyone. The young woman you are becoming, using your voice and writing talent, is incredible to witness. Isabel your joy and infectious energy light up a room. You show up to everything you do, all in, and I hope you forever foster your tenacious spirit. Leo, your Lego building next to me while I wrote sections of this book, brought me full circle to my why for writing. Stay curious and kind just as you are and may you keep your grateful, warm-hearted, and enthusiastic nature always. Ethan, my pandemic toddler, you brought more happiness than you will ever know, as we all were home to watch you grow and develop. Keep that jovial, loving, and imaginative energy you so freely give as a gift to all those around you. To my parents, for astutely showing me the way through their steadfast example of how to be in this world. You both exude generosity. To my partner, Mike, you are the glue, the rock, and the anchor, and I am so glad you invited me into your world all those years ago (and asked me for that mile while hiking the Grand Canyon).

—JAL

For women everywhere. May we know and champion the fierceness that lies within us. To my daughters, Thalia and Natasha, it is my life's honor to be your mother. You are my heart's song, God's purest grace, and everything beautiful in this world. Seize the world and soften it with your tenderness, light, and tantalizing goodness. To my mother, Anastasia, you are the strength of one thousand soldiers. If I have inherited even a morsel of your mothering, my love is bionic. To the women who lifted me up and carried me during this time, I walk because of you.

—EBL

This book is dedicated to my tribe. To Greg, my steadfast partner for life's voyage, you are an inspiration and the greatest support I could ever ask for. To Lydia, you made me a mom and reminded me of life's true joys: connecting with others and sharing love. I am continuously impressed with how you follow your passions, show kindness to others, and bring joy to the world with your friendly smile and quick wit. May you always manifest your dreams. To Evalyn, you are a brave soul, shining with brightness, which exudes wisdom—a blessing that healed my heart as your grandfather left the earth. I am so glad you are here to share a birthday with me. You spread sweetness and compassion wherever you go, and I am impressed with the amazing things you continue to accomplish. May you always embody and embrace your grandeur. To Henry, you are intelligent, mighty, and caring. You are a gift that keeps on giving with your tranquil spirit and wholesome nature. I am so delighted you were born and can't wait to see all you become. May you always live a life full of happiness. To Felicity, the youngest of our clan, your arrival was a lighthouse in the storm of the pandemic, bringing hope that things can and will be better. You are clever, resourceful, and ambitious. You share your cheer and sincere warmth with everyone you meet. May you thrive throughout your life. I love each of you for the unique wonders you are and am grateful for your presence in my life.

—KEP

Deepest appreciation to
Demeter's monthly Donors

DEMETER

Daughters
Summer Cunningham
Tatjana Takseva
Debbie Byrd
Fiona Green
Tanya Cassidy
Vicki Noble
Myrel Chernick

Sisters
Amber Kinser
Nicole Willey

Grandmother
Tina Powell